SKETCHING INTERIORS

FROM TRADITIONAL TO DIGITAL

SUINING DING, ASID, IDEC

Indiana University Purdue University
Fort Wayne, Indiana

Fairchild Books
New York

Executive Editor: Olga T. Kontzias
Assistant Acquisitions Editor: Amanda Breccia
Editorial Development Director: Jennifer Crane
Senior Development Editor: Joseph Miranda
Creative Director: Carolyn Eckert
Production Director: Ginger Hillman
Production Editor: Andrew Fargnoli
Copyeditor: Jean Ford
Ancillaries Editor: Noah Schwartzberg
Cover and Text Design: Tim Mackay
Cover Art: Suining Ding
Executive Director and General Manager: Michael Schluter

Library of Congress Catalog Card Number: 2010931054
ISBN: 978-1-56367-918-6
GST R 133004424
Printed in the United States of America

CH12.TP08

CONTENTS

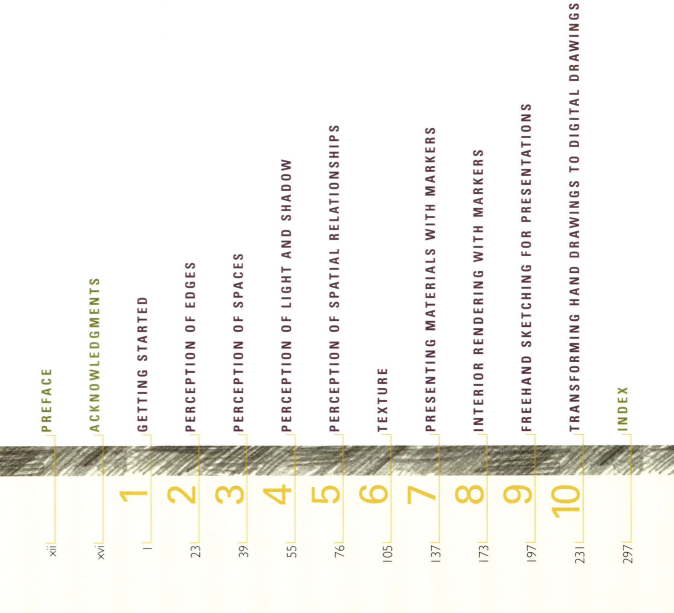

EXTENDED CONTENTS

PREFACE

UNIQUE FEATURES OF THE BOOK

Teaching sketching class is always fun and fascinating to me because I have the chance to observe how students learn to draw. Unlike many other people who believe that the ability to draw well is dependent on natural-born talent, I believe that all students can learn how to draw. With this thought in mind, I observed students' behaviors and listened to students' express their thoughts about drawing, and then, over many years of teaching, I explored a simple approach to teaching drawing class especially for sketching interiors with multiple media. I have experimented with various sequences and combinations of exercises. The exercises and instructions set out in this book have been designed specifically for students who have had no drawing experience before the class, ones who feel that they cannot draw, or those who may feel that they have little or no talent for drawing. It has been proved to be an effective method, in terms of student progress.

Freehand sketching is the language that conveys the design intent, perception, and the impressions of the designer. In my lectures and demonstrations, I tell my students that having drawing skills, aside from being a requirement for designers, can be a lifelong benefit. I always encourage my students to carry a sketchbook with them wherever they go—to create a journal or diary with sketches. You can express yourself in a different way—drawing by using the nonverbal language of art. Freehand sketching can create different images from what a camera can capture by integrating the designer's feelings and impressions.

This book contains several unique features that distinguish it from others, including the methods of editing freehand drawings by using Photoshop as well as introducing a new approach to teaching freehand sketching for interior design students based on Betty Edwards's *Drawing on the Right Side of the Brain* as a theoretical framework. In addition, another unique feature is that I use demonstrations and sample drawings as a thread throughout the book. Although Photoshop has been used widely for graphics, presenting the characteristics of freehand drawing in a digital drawing format is relatively new. I believe that the freehand lines of a drawing show a uniquely individual human thought and action process in an early schematic design phase. People recognize the human attributes and a personality present in freehand lines, marks, and strokes partly because of their imperfections. Therefore, introducing the method of presenting freehand drawing characteristics in a digital format became my passion. I believe that this technique provides more flexibility of graphic communication in the schematic design phase and represents a current industry standard.

PEDAGOGICAL FRAMEWORK OF THE BOOK

The book covers freehand sketching with multimedia, such as pencil, ink, and marker, as well as how to edit freehand drawings with Photoshop. The book provides step-by-step demonstrations that are very easy for beginning-level learners to follow.

Pedagogical features throughout the book are designed to assist teaching and enhance learning. To help explain the concepts and techniques, the book includes detailed demonstrations and exercises. Each chapter begins with a brief introduction, followed by demonstrations supporting the topic and then additional exercises to practice the techniques, a summary to study and recap the concepts learned, a list of key terms for a quick reference of what is covered in each chapter, and finally additional exercises. Many drawings are included for reference, inspiration, and practice. As mentioned earlier, *Drawing on the Right Side of the Brain* by Edwards was used as a theoretical framework to develop a freehand sketching pedagogy, based on the four perception skills: perception of edges, perception of spaces, perception of light and shadow, and perception of spatial relationships. During my years teaching freehand sketching classes, I found that this approach increases students' confidence in drawing and accelerates the learning progress in a sequential way that leads to the next level with solid basic concepts and skills. In addition, Nobel Prize winner and psychobiologist Roger W. Sperry's research on human brain-hemisphere functions affirmed this approach. His stunning findings that the human brain uses two different modes of thinking, one verbal, analytic, and sequential and one visual and perceptual, is the rational of this pedagogical framework.

ORGANIZATION OF THE BOOK

Because of the importance of freehand sketching in the interior design curriculum and the design process, this book is written for college-level freehand sketching courses as well as for design professionals who want to reinforce their sketching skills. It provides readers with more systematic demonstrations and exercises. The text is organized to enable an instructor to teach the drawing skills from very basic techniques that gradually move to the next level. It has been proven from my experience that this learning process not only sets a solid foundation for basic concepts, but also stimulates students' enthusiasm for drawing, especially for those who think that they do not have drawing talent.

The textbook is sequentially written and organized to develop the skills of traditional freehand sketching with multimedia before moving to digital drawing that highlights the characteristics of freehand sketching. The content is divided into ten chapters, as follows:

Chapter 1, "Getting Started," orients students about the best way to start, getting inspirations, and when and where to sketch, then provides an introduction to the concepts of perception in freehand drawing. Next it introduces the essential supplies needed for drawing in pencil, ink, and marker. The concept of using the left side and right side of the brain is also introduced, setting the stage for the four drawing perception skills discussed in following chapters. This chapter ends with a brief introduction about transforming freehand sketches to a digital format, with some example drawings that set the stage for a more detailed tutorial of this process in Chapter 10.

Chapter 2, "Perception of Edges," discusses the first perception skill—perception of edges. Contour drawings are explored in demonstrations and exercises. Line qualities are also introduced in this chapter. After finishing this chapter, students should be able to switch to the right side of the brain and use the senses of touch and sight to draw.

Chapter 3, "Perception of Spaces," introduces the second perception skill—perception of spaces. Negative space and positive form are discussed in this chapter. The composition of a drawing is introduced as well. The first attempt at shading for negative space with strokes is explored by demonstrations and exercises.

Chapter 4, "Perception of Light and Shadow," introduces the third perception skill—perception of light and shadow. In this chapter, how to observe tonal values are discussed. Shading and crosshatching techniques are demonstrated and explored in an array of exercises. In addition, drawing techniques, such as leaving white on the paper, drawing shadows, and defining form by surfaces are demonstrated in this chapter.

Chapter 5, "Perception of Spatial Relationships," discusses the fourth perception skill—perception of spatial relationships. Perspectives and proportions are two aspects of perception of spatial relationships. One-point perspective, two-point perspective, and three-point perspective are shown through demonstrations and exercises. Proportion is also demonstrated and discussed.

Chapter 6, "Texture," introduces the techniques of presenting texture with pencil and ink specifically for windows from both interior and exterior views, including the details of masonry, wood, roofs, and ceilings. How to draw shadows and openings is also covered, and drawing landscapes in ink is introduced.

Chapter 7, "Presenting Materials with Markers," covers basic techniques of using markers, such as presenting different values and materials. Rendering a window with drapery from an interior view is explored, as well as drawing materials such as masonry, wood, and furniture.

Chapter 8, "Interior Rendering with Markers," introduces the techniques of quick sketches with markers, using contrast and volume in the drawings. Color theory is also introduced in this chapter, specifically different color schemes and combinations; different drawing styles are explored as well, with examples.

Chapter 9, "Freehand Sketching for Presentations," introduces presentation techniques for floor plans, elevations, and perspective and isometric drawings. Entourages, such as human figures and trees, are discussed, and tree elevation and plan views are demonstrated.

Chapter 10, "Transforming Hand Drawings to Digital Drawings," gives a detailed tutorial for using Photoshop to transform freehand drawings to digital ones. Tips for editing digital images with Photoshop are provided. Emphasis is placed on how to keep the distinctive style and characteristics of a freehand drawing in a digital drawing through the many comparisons provided.

The Instructor's Guide available to instructors provides some additional demonstrations, exercises, and activities as well as individual and group projects to reinforce that both freehand sketching and digital drawing require constant practice to hone and refine drawing skills.

We all know that to be able to master the techniques of freehand sketching is critical for designers during the schematic design phase. The lines, strokes, and marks in freehand sketching made by designers are uncertain at the beginning of the design process and then become more determined and committed after design solutions are found. To be successful in the design field today, it is critically important to use freehand sketching as a catalyst to drawing with Photoshop. This new trend of using these digital tools that are changing and being enhanced constantly can only be implemented fully with basic drawing skills. I hope that the pedagogical approach in this book will help readers to become better designers who are able to sketch with multimedia. I believe that an excellent designer should also have excellent sketching skills that communicate design intents visually through graphics.

ACKNOWLEDGMENTS

I was thrilled to have the opportunity to write a textbook on freehand sketching, an important skill that is fundamental to interior design education and success in the profession.

I extend a heartfelt thank you to Olga Kontzias, executive editor, who deserves special mention for her dedicated support of interior design education and her belief in the need for this book. I am very grateful for her enthusiasm and guidance throughout the project. The book would not have become a reality without her assistance and trust. I am grateful for the team support and efforts provided by Fairchild Books. I extend heartfelt thanks to an experienced team of editors, including Joseph Miranda, senior development editor, for his encouragement, help, and thoroughness in the development process. I also extend thanks to Andrew Fargnoli, production editor, for his help and collaboration. Thanks to Carolyn Eckert, creative director, for her collaboration and talent. I am also grateful for the review and constructive criticism of proposal reviewers Deborah Brooks, SCAD; Bonnie DeBold, Art Institute of York, Pennsylvania; Laura Prestwood, Texas Christian University; Kathi VanderLaan, New England School of Art & Design; and development reviewers: Joan Dickinson, Radford University; Hans-Christian Lischewski, Mount Ida College; and Terry A. Postero, Buffalo State College.

My warmest thanks to my students whose very first critical feedback and project outcomes helped confirm and improve the pedagogical approach. Positive student evaluations encouraged me to continue to develop an easy-to-understand textbook during the book-writing process.

I am grateful to my parents, both natural scientists and professors, for giving me the freedom to pursue my education in architecture that combines arts and sciences, as well as interior design, which I have found to be my passion. Their inspirations in scientific research have been valuable to my scholarly activities in the design field. I also appreciate their unconditional support of my academic achievements in interior design education.

I am grateful to my family and friends who remain loyal and supportive while I spent many, many hours writing and drawing. I would not have the courage and determination to start another book and keep my creativeness in the writing odyssey without the unconditional support, encouragement, and trust of my dear friends. I would not have been able to write this book without the unconditional support of my husband, Fanyu, and my lovely daughter, Laura. I dedicate this book to my family and friends.

SKETCHING INTERIORS

1

GETTING STARTED

Freehand sketching is a means of communication for designers. Students and practitioners will frequently call upon freehand drawing skills to communicate ideas or support a point of view with clients, colleagues, and instructors. At other times, freehand drawings will be utilized to better understand aspects of one's own design or to refine them. Freehand sketching is used extensively in the design process, especially during the schematic design phase, which is for brainstorming and generating ideas. Designers need to effectively convey their ideas, both visually and verbally. There will also be times when these drawings are used to record a detail, a piece of furniture, an accessory, or a space. Therefore, the ability to draw and sketch becomes an important skill for designers because it supports a relaxed and fluid conversation among them and clients.

THE BEST WAY TO START

The best way to get started is get a sketchbook and your pencil ready to catch and record what you see on paper, express yourself, and learn to see the world around you better. Drawing is the best way to express and communicate your ideas to others visually. The most important step is to learn the "right way" to see objects around you.

GETTING INSPIRATION

Look through a variety of interior design and architectural books as well as interior design trade magazines that feature preliminary sketches, visit art galleries, and visit university departments of interior design, architecture, or art for different perspectives on inspiration. Pay attention to the way that space is presented through the lines, colors, and shadings. Those dimensions are central to some of the questions that you have to start asking: Did the designer use solid continuous lines everywhere? What are the color schemes and shadings? What kinds of lines are used to show different objects? You will start to notice that conceptual drawings do not always have to be technically perfect and the lines do not need to be straight or perfect. As a matter of fact, you will see double lines or even more lines for one single edge. Bert Dodson, author of *Keys to Drawing*, calls this "restating" the lines, and says, "Trial and error is essential in drawing. . . . Restatements demonstrate that the drawing is a vital, changing process" (Dodson, 1999). Therefore, sketching is the process of recording on paper what you see. Leaving the "incorrect" or "imperfect" lines on paper will make your drawing more vital.

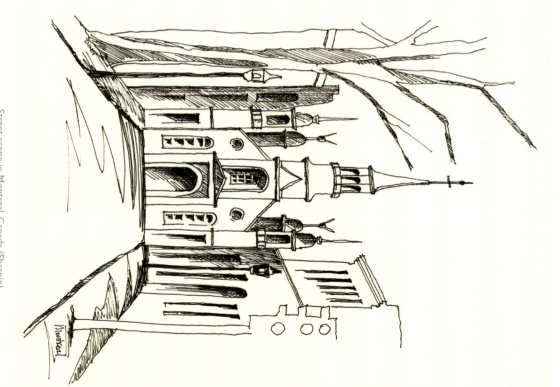

Street scene in Montreal, Canada (Sharpie)

1.1

1.2

The courtyard of The Pulitzer Foundation for the Arts museum designed by Tadao Ando, in St. Louis, Missouri (Sharpie)

WHEN AND WHERE TO DRAW

Carry your sketchbook with you all the time, wherever you travel. Draw what you see on a once-in-a-lifetime visit to a special location. Your sketchbook will be your journal or diary. Draw the most impressive and fascinat-

ing scenes you have seen. Freehand sketching can create different images from what a camera can create. Sketching can integrate the designer's feelings and impressions.

One of the keys for success in freehand sketching is practice. Most importantly, drawing technique is not only a skill for designers, but is also a lifelong benefit. The

following freehand sketches were drawn with a Sharpie: Figure 1.1 is a street scene in Montreal; Figure 1.2 is the courtyard of The Pulitzer Foundation for the Arts museum designed by Tadao Ando in St. Louis, Missouri; Figure 1.3 is the famous Gateway Arch in St. Louis, Missouri, and Figure 1.4 is the state capital building in Austin, Texas.

1.4

1.3

The state capital building in Austin, Texas (Sharpie)

The famous Gateway Arch in St. Louis, Missouri (Sharpie)

SKETCHING AND PERCEPTION

The way of perceiving an object is very important when you draw. An experienced designer or artist will see an object in a way that is different from the person who has never drawn before. The right way to perceive the object is to use the thought processes centered in the right side of your brain, not the left side, in which your numbering ability and analytical skills are dominant. In this book, how to perceive or see the object will be introduced at the very beginning. You will learn four basic drawing skills: perception of edges, perception of spaces, perception of light and shadow, and how to perceive spatial relationships.

THE ESSENTIAL ITEMS

Before you draw your very first stroke or line, you need to obtain the following basic items. These are essential, and as you develop more skills and become confident, you can obtain more and varied tools and materials.

Sketch Papers

Most drawing papers have a bit of tooth. That means they have subtle texture to catch and hold the pencil marks. However, some papers are quite smooth and allow you to get nice details. Sometimes, if you prefer to emphasize the rugged texture in your drawing, you may use a rougher textured paper, like watercolor paper: Strathmore, Canson, Morilla, Pentalic, and Aquabee are some good brands of drawing paper. Papers that are used for ink are generally very smooth. The Strathmore Bristol Smooth is particularly good.

Some types of sketch paper are suitable for multimedia use, and some are specialized for a particular media, such as marker sketchbooks. When you decide what kind paper to buy, you should consider the paper surface, along with the weight. Consider whether the sketch paper is multipurpose or designed to fit a specific group of media. A smooth surface is more suitable for line drawing, technical drawing, and finished art. A medium surface may be used for all dry media—including pencil, pastel, marker, ink, and Sharpie. There are different paper surfaces among medium surfaces. For ink or Sharpie, a smoother surface is better in order to have smooth and graceful lines.

Drawing paper is usually heavier in weight, and suitable for more developed work and finished drawings. Sketch paper is generally lighter in weight and more economical for preliminary drawings and practice work.

A toned paper, such as tan, gray, or gray-blue, sometimes can be very effective for certain sketching. It is available in loose sheets or in pads with a variety of shades. You may use a dark drawing tool like an ink pen or pencil to draw, and then come back with white pencil or white pastel to pick out highlights.

Sketchbook

Most sketchbooks are spiral-bound, allowing you to lay them out flat and work on both sides of the paper, but some are glued and/or clothbound along one edge. Choose one with a strong cardboard back or one with spiral binding. The advantage of using a clothbound sketchbook is that you can tear your drawings out without having the row of little round holes that spiral binding leaves. As for the size, a 9" × 12" sketchbook is recommended as the minimum size for class use. For travel purposes, a smaller sketchbook is easier to carry. Furthermore, smaller drawings are often easier to draw and take less time. Purchase a sketchbook like the ones in Figures 1.5a, 1.5b, or 1.6, and make sure the tooth (the coarseness and smoothness) on the surface of the paper in the sketchbook will absorb graphite and ink better than papers such as printing paper for laser printers.

1.5b Sketchbook

1.5a Sketchbook with colored pencils

Pencils

Pencils are important and should be good quality. Use 2B, 4B, 5B, and 6B. Usually, soft lead pencils are for freehand drawings and hard lead pencils are for drafting. Pencils with "B" grade are soft lead pencils, which are good for freehand drawing. A 6B pencil is much softer than a 2B pencil and produces a darker value. Pencils with "H" grade are hard lead pencils, which are good for drafting. Graphite pencils look like regular writing pencils that are sheathed in wood. Ebony pencils can be all lead with just a plastic coating. A flat sketch pencil (Figure 1.6) allows you to go for broader effects and areas of tone rather than line. You may try a 2B, which is reasonably soft.

Some drawing instruments are called mechanical pencils. They have refillable lead of various degrees of hardness from H to B. Mechanical pencils usually do not require a sharpener since the leads are so small in diameter, either 0.5 mm or 0.7 mm. Mechanical pencils are good for manual drafting. They do not work very well for freehand sketching.

Colored Pencils

Colored pencils are very useful. They can be used as combination media with markers. Colored pencils can draw details and create a broad range of values on the sketched object. Value refers to the continuum of brightness and darkness. The recommended brand of colored pencils are Prismacolor. They are wax based rather than graphite based and will not smear easily, so you can show the strokes. You will need to keep a pencil sharpener with you since the pencils lose their point rather quickly.

Eraser

A good eraser is needed. The best kind will be very soft, like a white plastic eraser. It won't damage your paper, leaves a minimum of crumbs, and gets rid of almost any pencil marks very nicely (Figure 1.7).

Kneaded Eraser

A kneaded eraser is similar to Play-Doh. You can knead it in your hand. A kneaded eraser works well to lift areas of tone or soft highlights from graphite or charcoal drawings.

1.6   Sketchbook with pencils and flat sketch pencil

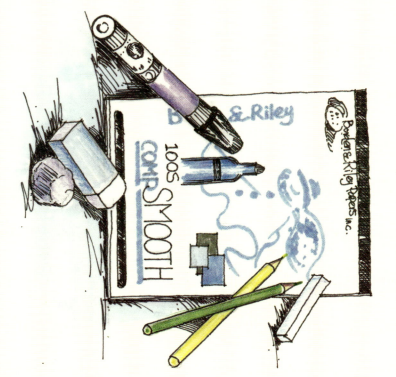

1.7   Marker papers with eraser, kneaded eraser, marker, colored pencils, and pastel

You can dip it on the shading area and make the shading lighter. The kneaded eraser can absorb a lot of graphite or charcoal power.

Pencil Sharpener

A small, handheld sharpener is fine (Figure 1.8). Figure 1.8 presents a simple pencil sharpener that has a plastic cover around it. The plastic case holds the pencil shavings. There are many different kinds of pencil sharpeners, including electric and battery operated ones.

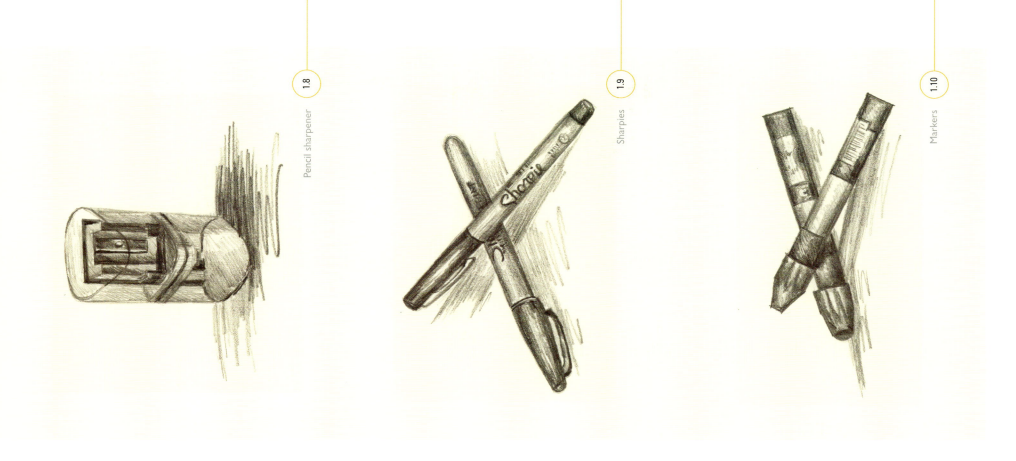

Ink Pens / Sharpies

For ink drawing, Sharpies are suggested (Figure 1.9). At lease two Sharpies are needed. One is an Ultra Fine Point Permanent Marker. This one can be used for thin lines. The second one is a Fine Point Permanent Marker. That one is for thick lines. You may also use other pens, such as uni-ball, Pilot Precise, or BIC Mark•it. Another type of ink pen is the Sakura Pigma® micron. It comes in different line weights, such as 0.01, 0.05, or 0.07.

Markers

There are several different brands of markers, such as Chartpak markers and Prismacolor markers. The colors chosen are based on your needs. Some recommended colors for Chartpak AD markers are Violet Light, Sapphire Blue, Sky Blue, Blue Glow, Willow Green, Grass Green, Nile Green, Pale Indigo, Maize, Buff, Sunset Pink, Suntan, Beige, Cool Gray 1, Cool Gray 5, and Brick Red, along with a Blender marker. (Figure 1.10). You also can use Prismacolor markers, which have thick (chiseled shape) and thin tips at each end of the marker. A thick tip (chiseled shape) allows you to draw broad strokes and a thin tip allows you to draw thin strokes. The recommended colors are Cool Grey 20%, Warm Grey 20%, Warm Grey 30%, Light Peach, Light Walnut, Goldenrod, and Sienna Brown.

Marker Papers

The recommended marker paper is 100% pure rag marker paper from Borden & Riley. The size can be 14" × 17" (50 sheets) or 24" × 36" (50 sheets). Another recommended marker paper is Graphics 360 from Bienfang Design series. It is a 100% rag, nonbleeding translucent marker paper. It retains true color with permanent as well as watercolor markers.

DRAWING WITH CONFIDENCE: THE VERY FIRST STROKE

Before you start the first drawing in your sketchbook, try out your pencils and discover the difference between a 2B and a 6B pencil. Look at the shadings in Figure 1.11. Relax your wrist, press harder at the begin-

ning and then gradually release the pressure. With practice, you will draw shading in different brightness and darkness. You will feel that a 2B pencil has a harder lead than a 6B pencil. You also will feel that when you press harder, you will get a darker value with all these pencils. For creating a darker value, a softer lead pencil is better than a hard lead pencil.

1.11

2B

3B

4B

5B

6B

9B

9B

Different weight pencil strokes

Getting familiar with your new tools is important before you start your first drawing. Try your very first stroke with each of these new tools and become confident using them. Draw strokes and make marks with each one. Lay down areas of tone. Draw different lines.

Have fun! And keep practicing. The key is to relax your wrist and become confident with pencils in order to overcome any fear of drawing. The very first step to success in drawing is to loosen up. A tight person will not be able to succeed in drawing because of the fear. So remember this, and enhance your drawing techniques; enjoy it.

EXERCISE

EXPLORING YOUR TOOLBOX

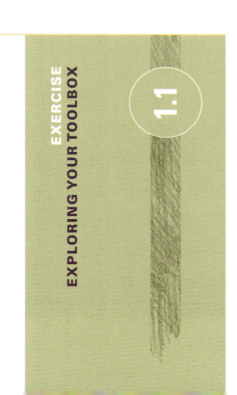

1.1

YOUR BRAIN: LEFT SIDE AND RIGHT SIDE

During my years of teaching freehand sketching, I heard many frustrated students say, "I just can't draw." Those students think that they do not have any drawing talent at all. I explain to them that they have to be able to see the object with the "right perception." If you are interested in learning more about how to see the object with the right perception, which involves shifting from the left side to the right side of your brain, I recommend the book *Drawing on the Right Side of the Brain* by Betty Edwards. Since this book is written specifically for interior design students, the emphasis is on how to sketch an interior space instead of on drawing a portrait or landscape.

Seeing and Perceiving Objects

According to Edwards, the left side of your brain dominates your abilities of language, logical thinking, memory, and math. The right side of your brain dominates your abilities of visualization, creativity, music, and graphic art. Therefore, in order to be able to draw, you need to switch your mode of perceiving from left side (L-mode) to right side (R-mode). The very first step to learning how to draw is to learn how to see the object. You will be able to draw only with the right-side perception skill. There are four basic perception skills introduced in Edwards's book. The first perception skill is how to see the edges of objects. The second is how to see the spaces, while the third is how to see lights and shadows. The fourth skill is how to see the spatial relationships (Edwards, 1999, p. xviii).

What is the magical mystery of drawing ability? It is to be able to shift your mode to the right side of your brain and be able to see or perceive objects in the special way in which an experienced artist sees.

Upside-Down Drawing: Shifting to R-Mode

When you see things that are upside down, they do not look the same and are not familiar to you. The reason is that in upright orientation we can recognize familiar things, name them, and categorize them by matching our preexisting and stored memories and concepts. However, when the image is upside down, the visual clues do not work. Even well-known faces are difficult to recognize and name because our brain is confused by the visual clues (Edwards, 1999).

Since the left side of your brain does not easily recognize familiar faces and other objects in an upside-down-orientation drawing, we can use this gap in the abilities of the left side of the brain to allow the right side of the brain to have a chance to take over for the drawing task (Edwards, 1999). Figure 1.12 is an example of an upside-down drawing of the famous musician Ludwig van Beethoven.

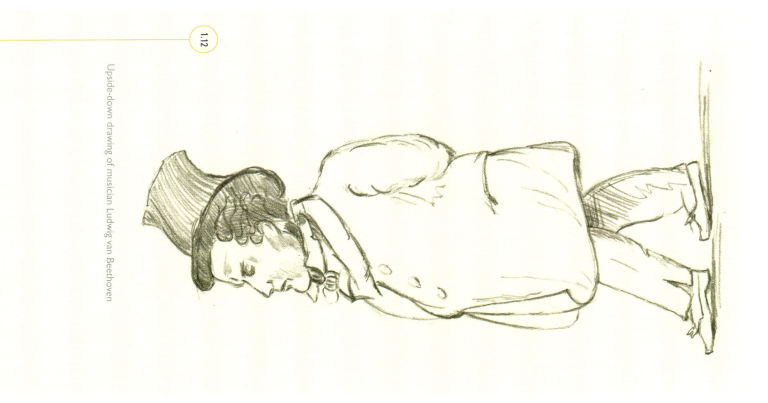

1.12

Upside-down drawing of musician Ludwig van Beethoven

Copy the image shown in Figure 1.12, viewing it exactly the way it is shown on the page. (Tip: You may play music if you like. As you shift into the right side of your brain, you may feel that the music fades out.) When you start your upside-down drawing, do not turn your drawing right side up until you finish it. Turning your drawing right side up will enable you to shift back to the left side of the brain. Start anywhere you wish. Do not try to figure out what you are drawing and do not try to identify and name the objects. Simply copy the lines shown in the figure.

Now turn your drawing around 180 degrees and view it. Are you surprised with the results? I think you will be pleased with your drawing, especially if you thought you would not be able to draw at all.

EXERCISE
UPSIDE-DOWN DRAWING

1.2

The objective of this exercise is to experience the conflicting modes and to shift from the left side to the right side of your brain.

In this exercise, you will drop your L-mode and let your R-mode take over the task of perceiving the image, which is just what we want in drawing.

Choose one of your favorite photos and place it upside down. The photo could be a portrait of a famous person or a friend. Draw the portrait with pencil. After you finish it, turn the photo right side up and compare it with the drawing that you just did.

The objective of this exercise is to experience the process of dropping the left side of the brain way of thinking, which means forgetting all the names of objects, and using the right side of the brain. Do not worry about the perspective of the space or the perspective of the objects in the space.

Choose one of your favorite interior space photos from a book or magazine. Turn it upside down. Use your pencil to draw the room. Forget all the names of the furniture and accessories in the room and do not worry about the perspective of the space. Just draw what you see. After you finish the drawing, compare it with the photo.

EXERCISE

UPSIDE-DOWN DRAWING

(INTERIOR SPACE PHOTOS)

1.4

SKETCHING INTERIORS

As mentioned earlier in this chapter, you will need to learn four perception skills in order to be able to draw a good interior sketch. These four skills are (1) perceiving edges, which is the contour drawing, (2) perceiving spaces, which is the negative space drawing, (3) perceiving lights and shadows, which is the value drawing, and (4) perceiving spatial relationships and proportions, which is per-

spective. Obtaining the first two skills will enable you to see objects in a right way, which means using the right side of your brain. The third skill will allow you to draw the object in a three-dimensional form and convey the sense of distance. The fourth skill will ensure that you draw the space and object with the correct perspective and proportion. The four drawing skills will be introduced in subsequent chapters. You will also learn how to use different media in addition to pencil,

such as ink and markers. After you become familiar with skills and develop confidence, you will be able to master interior sketching. Figures 1.13, 1.14, and 1.15 are examples of using these skills. These quick sketches present a schematic design for a volleyball club. Figure 1.13 is a reception area; Figure 1.14 is the coaches' office; Figure 1.15 is the entrance lobby.

1.13

Reception area of a volleyball club (marker, ink, colored pencil)

Coaches' office of volleyball club (marker, ink, colored pencil)

Lobby entrance of volleyball club (marker, ink, colored pencil)

FROM FREEHAND SKETCHING TO DIGITAL DRAWING

Freehand sketching presents the sense of human "touch" and the unique individual manner and style. Freehand sketching also presents the process of creative thinking. All those characteristics of freehand sketch-

ing are desired qualities for drawings in the design process. Careful use of transformation techniques in Photoshop can maintain these characteristics in digital drawings. The following are digital drawings (Figures 1.16–1.19) that were edited by Photoshop. These drawings maintain the sense of human touch by keeping freehand lines and strokes. They also can present some kind of realism

by using real photos, such as incorporating a photo of the sky. Compare these digital drawings to the original drawings in Figures 1.1–1.4. Chapter 10 will show many more examples and give you the tools for digital drawing and editing procedures. The editing process is very simple. It creates more polished digital drawings that maintain the characteristics of freehand sketching.

Digital drawing of Montreal street scene created using Photoshop

1.16

1.17

Digital drawing of the courtyard of The Pulitzer Foundation for the Arts museum in St. Louis, Missouri, created using Photoshop

Digital drawing of the famous Gateway Arch in St. Louis, Missouri, created using Photoshop

1.18

Digital drawing of the state capital building in Austin, Texas, created using Photoshop

SUMMARY

In this chapter, you:

- Were introduced to essential drawing tools and materials.

- Have drawn your first strokes in pencil.

- Learned that artists perceive their objects by switching their mode of perceiving from the left side of the brain to the right side.

- Were exposed to digital drawings created from ink sketches.

Drawing upside down is an exercise in experiencing modes of conflict and switching to the R-mode. Practice with more upside-down exercises and get used to using your R-mode when you are drawing.

KEY TERMS

Colored Pencils	Left Side of the Brain	Pencils
Eraser/Kneaded Eraser	Marker Papers	Pencil Sharpener
Ink Pens (Sharpies)	Markers	Right Side of the Brain	Sketchbook
			Sketch Papers

ADDITIONAL EXERCISES

1. Turn Figure 1.12 right-side up. Draw Figure 1.12 in your sketchbook. After you finish it, compare it to the experience of drawing it upside down and compare the two drawings.

References

Dodson, Bert, Keys to Drawing. Cincinnati, OH: North Light Books, 1990. Edwards, Betty, Drawing on the Right Side of the Brain. New York: Jeremy P. Tarcher/Putnam, a member of Penguin Putnam, Inc., 1999.

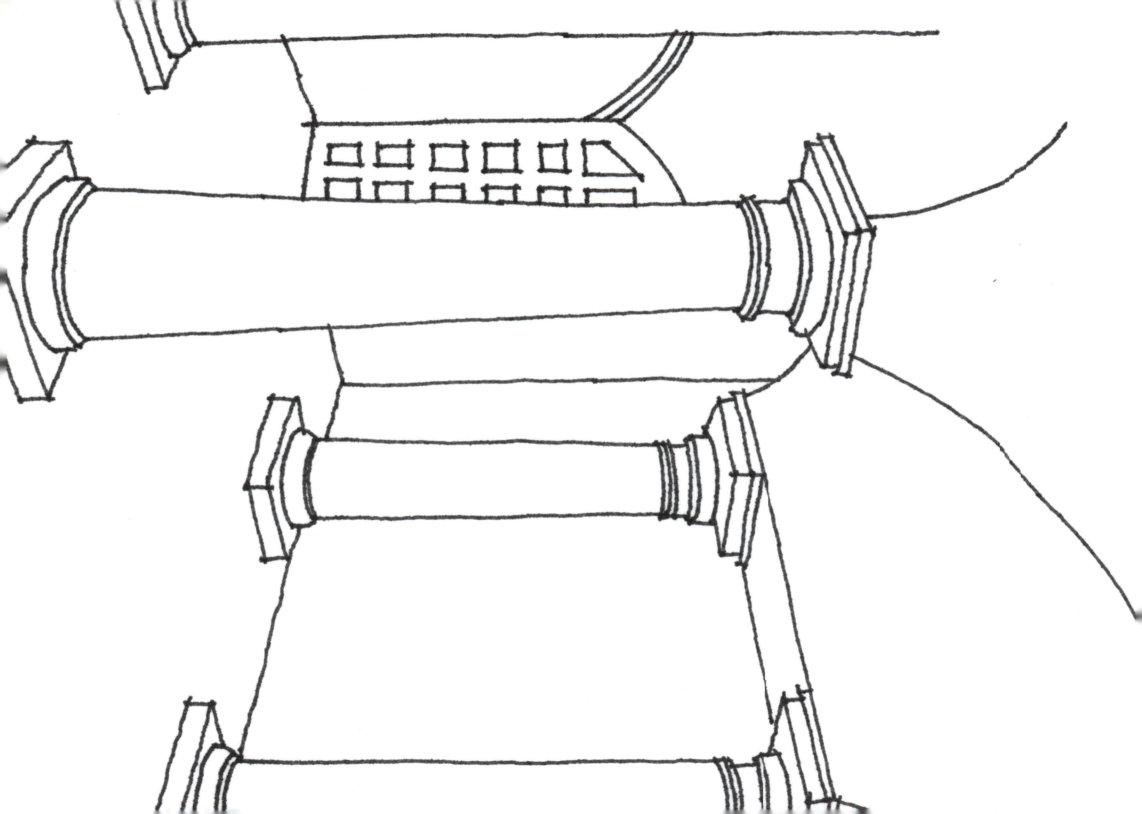

2

PERCEPTION OF EDGES

CONTOUR DRAWING

As mentioned before, the first drawing skill to learn is how to perceive the edges of objects. The right way to see an object is to switch from L-mode to R-mode and use the right side as opposed to the left side of your brain. You have used upside-down drawings to experience this process. In this chapter, you will try another method to force you to drop your L-mode and shift to your R-mode completely.

Contour drawing is the place where most drawing lessons start. Contour drawing is following the visible edges of a shape. The contour presents the outermost edges of a form, as well as dramatic changes of plane within the form. With contour drawing, you need to focus on the edges—the outside of an object or the line made by a fold or pattern. The line that goes across an object is called a cross-contour. You do not need to put any shading on a contour drawing. Different line weights will make the contour stand out on the paper (if it is a strong, dark line) or stay unobtrusive on the paper (if it is light or thin). This technique is useful when you are trying to give the impression of something being close or far away.

Contour drawings were introduced by a revered art teacher, Kimon Nicolaides,

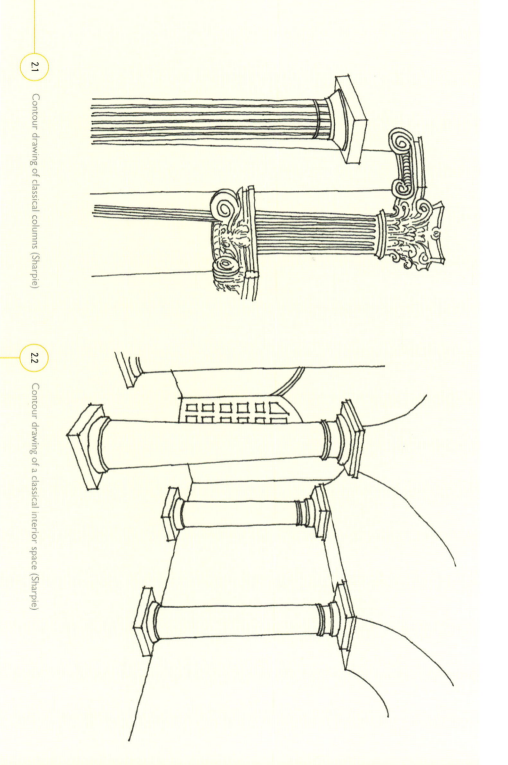

2.1 Contour drawing of classical columns (Sharpie)

2.2 Contour drawing of a classical interior space (Sharpie)

in his 1941 book, *The Natural Way to Draw.* Nicolaides felt that the reason the contour method improved students' drawing was that it caused students to use the senses of sight and touch. This method has been used widely by art teachers. Betty Edwards used this concept in her teaching and her book *Drawing on the Right Side of the Brain.* She suggested an alternate possibility for the method's success, which is that the L-mode rejects the complex perceptions of spatial information, therefore allowing access to R-mode processing. Thus, contour drawing is not suited for left side of the brain thinking. Contour drawing uses the senses of touch and sight, which are functions of the right side of your brain—exactly what is needed when you draw. In later chapters, you will learn how to sketch interiors with more complex skills, such as perspective and proportion. Therefore, using the right way to perceive interior space is critical. Contour drawings will give you training in how to use the senses of touch and sight when you draw.

DEMONSTRATION: CONTOUR DRAWINGS

There are many objects that make good subjects for contour drawings. For example, flowers in a vase, a piece of furniture, and of course, any interior space or architecture will make a good subject for contour drawings. When you choose an object for contour drawing, remember these features:

1. Use an object with complex curves, for example, a classical interior space or architecture as well as classical furniture.

2. View the object from unfamiliar angles.

3. Imagine that the point of the pencil is your fingertip, which you carefully run around the edge of the object that you are drawing. Do not look at the drawing too often. Keep your eyes on the object as much as possible while you draw. Contour drawing is good training because it teaches you to look at the object carefully using the right side of your brain and draw it simply. Figures 2.1—2.4 show some examples of contour drawings. Figure 2.1 is a contour drawing of classical column orders (Doric, Ionic, and Corinthian). Figure 2.2 is a contour drawing of a simple interior space in classical architectural style; Figures 2.3 and 2.4 show two Baroque-style interior spaces.

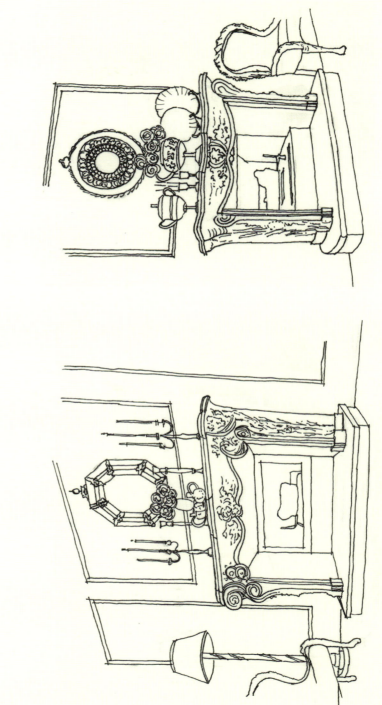

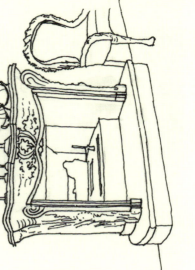

2.4   Contour drawing of a Baroque-style interior space (Sharpie)

2. PERCEPTION OF EDGES   25

2.3   Contour drawing of a Baroque-style interior space (Sharpie)

2.5

Contour drawing of a hand (Sharpie)

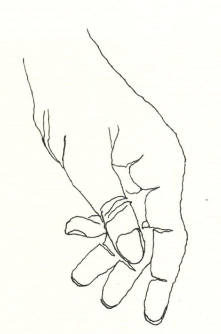

Contour drawing of a hand (Sharpie)   2.6

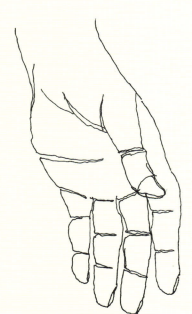

The following are simple demonstrations. The purpose of doing them is to train your eye to see edges of an object.

1. Use your left hand as a model if you are a right-handed person. Set your left hand at a position that you are comfortable with and relax.

2. Relax your right hand as well. Look at your left hand while you are keeping your pencil on the paper. Try to trace the edges and folds of your left hand as if your fingers were touching them.

3. Start with the longest lines or edges.

4. Forget the names of each part of your hand. Just record what you see as your eye tracks the direction of the edge of your hand. When the edge changes the direction, so does your pencil.

5. Move your pencil slowly. Observe the changes of direction on your hand and record these changes on paper.

6. You can change the position of your left hand and then draw each of these positions of your left hand. Figures 2.5 and 2.6 are two examples of contour drawings of a hand.

7. You can start by using your pencil. After you finish your contour drawing, you can use your Sharpie to trace the contour drawing. The recommended pencil is a soft lead pencil, such as 4B or 5B.

CONTOUR DRAWING DEMONSTRATION #2

1. Use a piece of furniture as a model, for example, a chair or a table that has complex curves. Figure 2.7 is a contour drawing of a chair in a classical-style interior space.

2. Relax yourself and your hand as well. Look at the furniture while you are keeping your pencil on the paper. Try to trace the edges and folds of the furniture as if your fingers were touching them.

3. Start with the longest lines or edges.

4. Move you pencil slowly. Observe the changes on the furniture and record these changes on paper.

5. Forget the names of each part of the object, such as cushion and backing. Just record what you see. Use your eye to track the direction of the edge of the furniture. When the edge of the furniture changes direction, so should your pencil.

6. After you finish your contour drawing, use a Sharpie to trace the drawing.

7. You will be surprised at the results when you have finished this contour drawing and experienced this method of object perception.

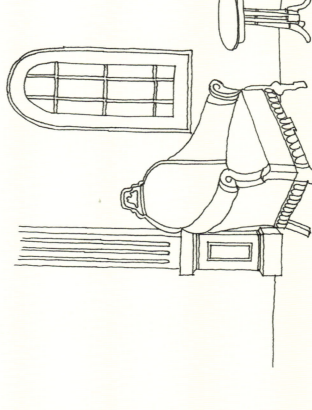

2.7   Contour drawing of a chair in a classical-style interior space (Sharpie)

EXERCISE 2.1

CONTOUR DRAWING—SIMPLIFYING AN OBJECT WITH THE GROUPING-LINE TECHNIQUE

You can draw interior accessories for contour drawings, such as a vase with flowers (Figures 2.8 and 2.9). The lines of a contour drawing should be smooth and graceful. The key is to be loose and relaxed. You do not need to draw every single leaf or petal when looking at a vase of flowers. You can use the grouping-line technique to simplify the object. You can learn just as much by drawing with a thick line that groups its way slowly around a relatively complex shape. Use a soft pencil, such as 4B or 5B, when you try to simplify the object with the grouping-line technique. Once again, think of the point of your pencil as your fingertip moving around the edge of the shape. Move your pencil very slowly; imagine you are using your finger to touch the object. This is another kind of contour drawing method that develops your ability to visualize and record shapes simply.

2.8

Contour drawing of flowers in vase (Sharpie)

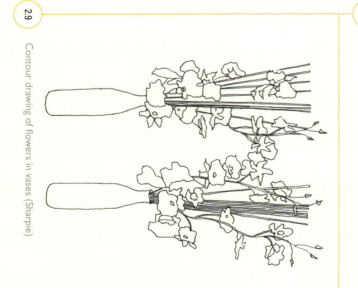

2.9

Contour drawing of flowers in vases (Sharpie)

Choose a photo of a classical interior space or classical architecture to practice this exercise. Figure 2.10 is a contour drawing of a Gothic interior space. There are many architectural components in the space, such as vaults, columns, and pointy-arch windows. You can start drawing with big, scribbly lines. This is another useful technique for contour drawings, especially for beginners. Again, be loose and relax! Use a soft pencil, such as 4B or even 5B. Draw rapidly, swinging your wrist and moving around the forms with bold strokes. You may go over the lines as many times as you want. You can scribble back and forth. Naturally, you will find that you visualize your subject as a series of simple geometric shapes. This technique is important because it is critical for you to know how to simplify your subject into geometric shapes. Figure 2.11 is a contour drawing of a big, open interior space with a lot of classical architectural components. You can visualize a Corinthian capital as a thin, square plate form on top and a cylinder that is big at the upper portion and small at the lower portion; all the columns can be visualized as cylinders.

EXERCISE

CONTOUR DRAWING—SCRIBBLING A COMPLEX FORM TO A SIMPLE GEOMETRIC FORM

2.2

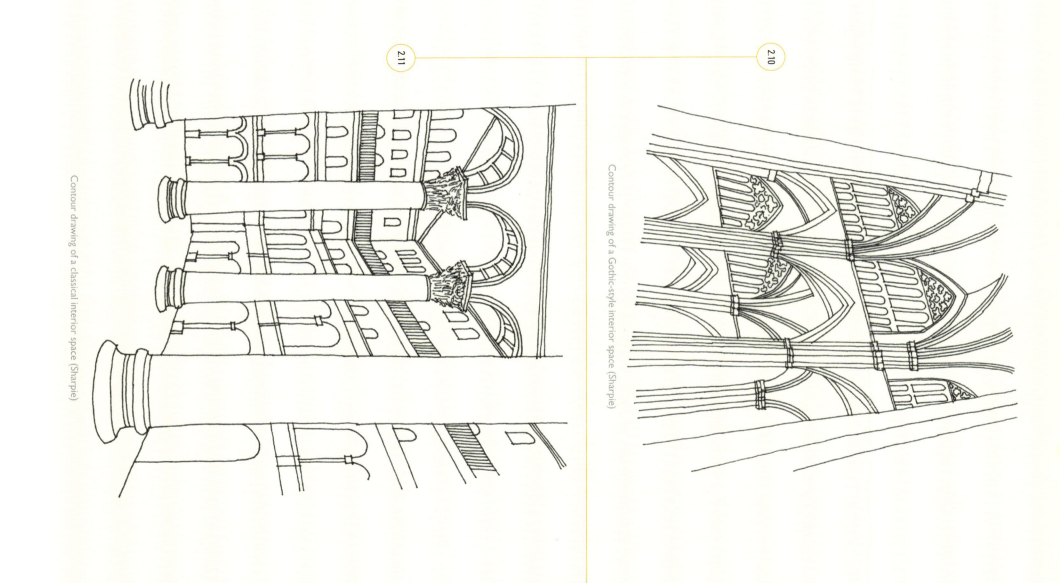

2.11

Contour drawing of a classical interior space (Sharpie)

2.10

Contour drawing of a Gothic-style interior space (Sharpie)

EXPLORING LINES

A line is a mark made by a pencil, pen, marker, or other writing instrument, and is often defined as a moving dot. It has length and width. Variety in the thickness of lines creates interest in a drawing. Some lines are thick; some are thin; many lines have both thin and thick qualities. Lines can be expressive because of their endless variety. Some lines can be described as nervous, soft, heavy, wavy, or exciting for their qualities. Using a variety of lines in your drawing can also add visual interest and imply depth, movement, light, and so on.

Quality of Lines

One extraordinary aspect of drawings by the famous masters is the quality of the lines they use to present the planes and roundness of surfaces. Every line is drawn deliberately. It has a clean beginning and a clean end. Where the lines are meant to be parallel they are parallel. Where they are meant to be curved they are all curved with regularity. Every one of those lines is doing its own job, no more and no less. It is rare to ever see a squiggle or a tick at the end of the line. Therefore, the quality of lines is an important aspect of all drawings. Leonardo da Vinci's drawings are excellent examples of line qualities. Looking at his drawings his lines are very precise and very smooth. Details in drawings were presented by using bold lines to barely visible lines. Da Vinci captured the light and darkness of the object by using thickness of the lines in his drawings. Appreciating masterpieces of drawings will help you in understanding drawing techniques and getting inspirations.

Here are some basic line qualities that you should use in your drawings. The very first key point is to make your line smooth and graceful, which means you draw lines with looseness and relaxation.

1. The first line quality is that the line weight should be different from the beginning to the end (see Figure 2.12). Hold your pencil and relax. Press harder when you first touch the paper. Then lift your pencil a bit and keep drawing. Then press harder again. You will get a line that has different line weights.

2. The second line quality is that the line is broken with intention. Sometimes you will see a little dot in the line. It is called skip line. See the examples in Figure 2.12. You will use a skip line in many cases when you sketch. Your eyes will fill in the break and you will see the skip line like a continuous line.

3. The third line quality is that the line looks like it is dancing on the paper. See the examples in Figure 2.12. It is called an exciting line by some artists. To draw an exciting line, you have to twist your pencil and let it dance on the paper. Once more, be loose and relax! The exciting line can be used for sketching bushes or trees.

Line quality, continued

In addition, there are several rules of thumb for line qualities. First, lines need to be deliberate and confident. That can be achieved by the artist's determination at the beginning of drawing a line. Second, lines need to be crossed at corners when two lines intersect. Leaving a gap at the corner is not a good practice. Third, for mass profile (or hatching area), 45-degree strokes usually are applied. The stroke technique will be discussed in Chapter 4 in detail.

No matter what kind of line quality that you are aiming for, the line needs to be smooth and graceful—loose and relaxed (Figure 2.12).

Contour drawing is line drawing, which is pretty much what it sounds like: using lines to capture objects. There is no shading or brightness and darkness on the drawing of the object. Therefore, there is no sense of three-dimensional form. However, practicing contour drawings will train you to perceive the object.

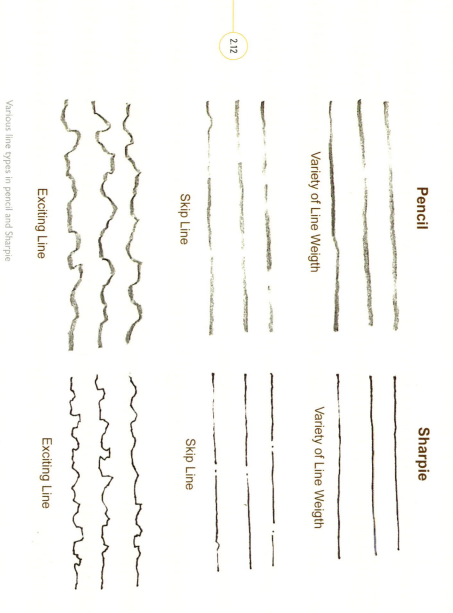

2.12

Various line types in pencil and Sharpie

Pencil

Variety of Line Weigth

Skip Line

Exciting Line

Sharpie

Variety of Line Weigth

Skip Line

Exciting Line

FROM CONTOUR DRAWING TO DIGITAL DRAWING

Contour drawing is the first step of the transformation from hand drawing to digital drawing. The following figures (Figures 2.13, 2.14, and 2.15) are three examples that have been created in Photoshop. (Compare them to Figures 2.4, 2.7, and 2.11.) Usually the lines in contour drawings are closed lines. It makes the editing process for drawings easier. Since contour drawings are made freehand, they present all the characteristics of freehand drawing, including imperfections. Detailed procedures are described in Chapter 10.

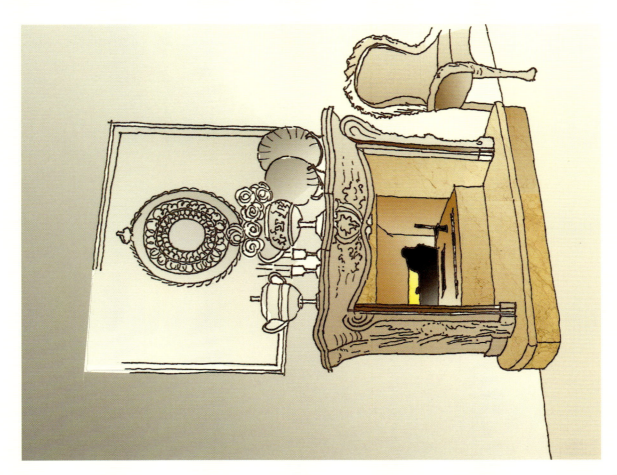

TIPS AND HINTS

- Be loose and relaxed.
- Perceive the object with your senses of sight and touch.
- Use different line weights and other line qualities in drawing.
- Exposed to digital drawings that were created from contour drawing.

2.14

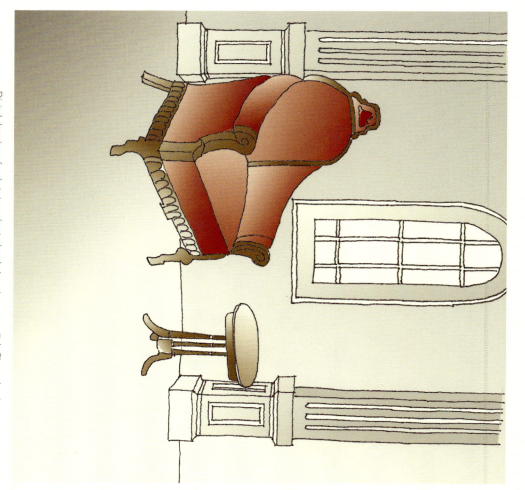

Digital drawing of a chair in a classical-style interior space (ink, Photoshop)

Digital drawing of a classical interior space (ink, Photoshop)

SUMMARY

This chapter introduces the concept of contour drawings. It is the first drawing skill that you will learn—how to perceive the edges of objects. You have explored lines of different types and qualities.

After you have finished this chapter, you are able to understand:

- The concept of contour drawings.

- Why contour drawings suit the right side of the brain.

- How to perceive the edges.

- Line qualities.

You will also be able to:

- Switch to R-mode and use the senses of touch and sight to draw.

- Draw line drawings with different line types and qualities.

KEY TERMS

Contour Drawings	Line Qualities	Sense of Sight	Thick Line
Exciting Line	Line Types	Sense of Touch	Thin Line
Grouping Lines	Scribbling	Skip Line	

ADDITIONAL EXERCISES

1. Draw a contour drawing of your hand. You may change the position of your hand.

2. Choose a piece of classical furniture and draw it using the contour drawing method. You can use either a three-dimensional piece of furniture or a photo.

3. Choose a photo of an interior space or architecture. Draw it using the contour drawing method. Remember to use your sense of sight to trace the edge of the object.

4. Create a contour drawing using a vase of flowers or a plant as your model.

Reference

Edwards, Betty, *Drawing on the Right Side of the Brain*. New York: Jeremy P. Tarcher/Putnam, a member of Penguin Putnam, Inc., 1999.

3

PERCEPTION OF SPACES

NEGATIVE SPACE AND POSITIVE FORM

After you understand and practice contour drawing, and learn how to perceive the edges of an object, you are ready to learn how to perceive spaces. You know that when you draw, you will have to drop your L-mode completely and use your R-mode. When beginners start to draw, they have preconceived stereotypes about objects. For example, drawing a piece of furniture, like a coffee table, beginners know that the coffee table has a top and four legs equal in length. However, this kind of information essentially will not help beginners to draw the table.

In teaching beginners to draw, many art educators use the method of instructing them just to perceive the spaces around the object. Betty Edwards provides an explanation of why this method works. As she stated in *Drawing on the Right Side of the Brain*, "I believe that it's because you don't know anything in a verbal sense about these spaces" (p. 18). Therefore, you will be able to see spaces clearly and draw them correctly because you do not have preexisting, memorized symbols for space-shapes. In this chapter, you will learn how to perceive spaces, as well as the concept of composition, which is an important component in sketching. You

also will explore some basic shading/stroke skills for the negative space, which is known as a toned background.

WHAT ARE NEGATIVE SPACE AND POSITIVE FORM?

This concept is easy to understand. In the drawing of a chair, for example, the chair is the positive form and the background behind the chair and the empty space formed between different parts of the chair (for example, the legs) are the negative space. The negative space includes all the empty areas. When you start a negative space drawing, instead of observing the positive shape of an object, you observe and draw the empty shapes formed between different parts of the object, or between one

edge of the object and a boundary. This may include any background detail. By drawing the background spaces or shapes between the edge of the object and the opposing edge or boundary, the positive form of the object is "left out," resulting in a negative space drawing.

Defining Composition

Composition is a very important component in drawing. You may draw the object or sketch the interior space with appropriate color, and accurate perspective and line qualities, but if the composition of the drawing is not good, it will destroy the entire drawing. Therefore, it is very critical to understand the composition concept at the beginning of the learning process. The rule of thumb for judging whether the drawing has a good composition is to see whether the positive

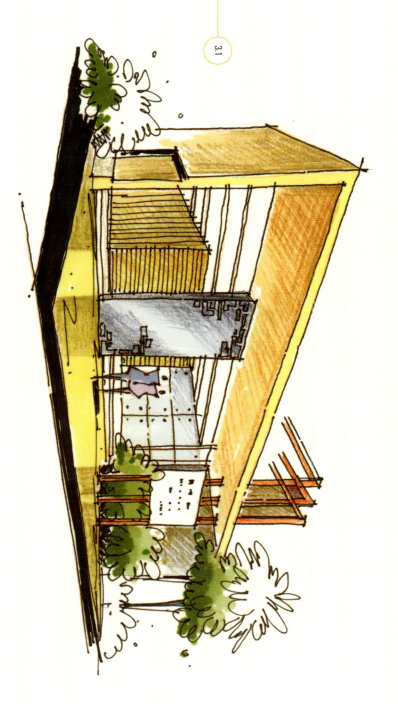

Retail storefront design (marker, Sharpie, colored pencil)

Drawing composition analysis (marker, ink)

32

forms and negative spaces are balanced. In drawing, the positive form is the focal point that has strong contrast with details. You want to attract the viewer's attention to it. The negative spaces become the background. You will need to make the background support the positive forms. In order to balance the positive forms and negative spaces you can use color, shape, and visual weight. The concept of balance here does not refer to absolute balance, which is symmetrical or identical. It is, in a sense, unity achieved by different shapes of positive forms and colors as well as different values (darkness and brightness).

BALANCE

The main characteristic of a good composition is that it creates a feeling of balance in the viewer's mind. This balance includes two aspects:

Balance of position. This means that the forms and spaces in the drawing should be balanced relative to the vertical and the horizontal axes going through the center of the page.

Balance of value. The darkness and brightness should balance each other out in an overall sense. In other words, having too much black on one side or a complete lack of it is not recommended.

FOCAL POINT

One common compositional mistake is that the viewer's eye is led in a direction away from the center of interest. Usually, the viewer's eye tends to enter a drawing from the left (just as you read from left to right). Therefore, a good composition often has an entry point on the left of the drawing,

and from there leads the viewer's eye to the focal point.

DETAIL

The focal point should also be the area where you add the most detail and strong contrast to your drawing. Areas deemed less important can be less developed and left to be finished by the viewer's imagination.

Figures 3.1 and 3.2 demonstrate good examples of composition. The sketches are drawn with markers, colored pencils, and ink. The focal point is the entrance, which is highlighted by the stone wall and two human figures. In order to balance the effect of perspective, taller architectural elements and trees were drawn on the right side. The drawing is well balanced.

Viewfinder (pencil)

3.3

Viewfinder

Sketching using a viewfinder can help you to determine what will be included in your drawing in order to achieve a better composition. A viewfinder is a mechanical aid. It is simply a piece of cardboard with a rectangular opening (about 1 × 1.25) that corresponds roughly to the proportions of your drawing. You can make the opening bigger but still within the same proportion of your drawing (Figure 3.3).

By focusing, before you begin, on the main object that you would like to draw, by moving it up and down or from left to right, you can select what you think is the most pleasing arrangement. The margin of the viewfinder blocks off enough of the scene to allow you to concentrate on what you see through the opening.

You only use the viewfinder during the planning of the composition. You will have to squint or close one eye when focusing and varying the distance when holding the viewfinder, depending on the number of objects you wish to include in your drawing.

If you do not have a viewfinder that is made from cardboard, you can use your hands to frame a viewfinder. What you can do is use your thumbs and the index fingers of both hands. The palm of your left hand faces you, and the palm of your right hand faces you, and the palm of your right hand palm faces outward.

Shading with Strokes

Shading is another essential concept in drawing. It will be discussed in detail in Chapter 4 when light and shadow are introduced. However, since shading is very important in sketching and helpful for creating background (negative space), you will begin to master this process by attempting some initial strokes. A pencil is a good tool to start with. In most cases, 45-degree angled pencil strokes will work, except if you are trying to suggest directions of the surface. Sometimes you may pile up your pencil strokes on top of others with different angles. This will make the area darker and can create a smoother texture. This is also called crosshatching. See Chapter 4 for more details.

Shading is the act of creating an accurate range of values with smooth transitions. Value means brightness and darkness. Shading can present a more accurate sense of how light might fall on an object. By applying more or less pressure to the pencil, you can make values darker or lighter. You also can

use a variety of pencils to produce a variety of values.

Shading works best when there is an organized manner in which strokes are drawn on the paper. Strokes made in one direction will help to create a uniform surface to your shading. If your strokes are too visible, you can shade across your first layer with a second layer of strokes in a different direction to make your shading smoother.

Edges are important in shading. To create a strong edge, the strokes should not go

beyond the shape. In order to have a crisp clean edge, stroke away from the edge of the shape and then clean up by stroking carefully along the edge of the shape.

Figure 3.4 shows three simple geometric forms: cube, cone, and sphere. The cube is drawn by shading with 45-degree strokes. The cone is drawn by crosshatching, which is created by changing the angle of the second layer of strokes. The sphere is drawn by crosshatching as well. The difference is that the strokes are curved lines.

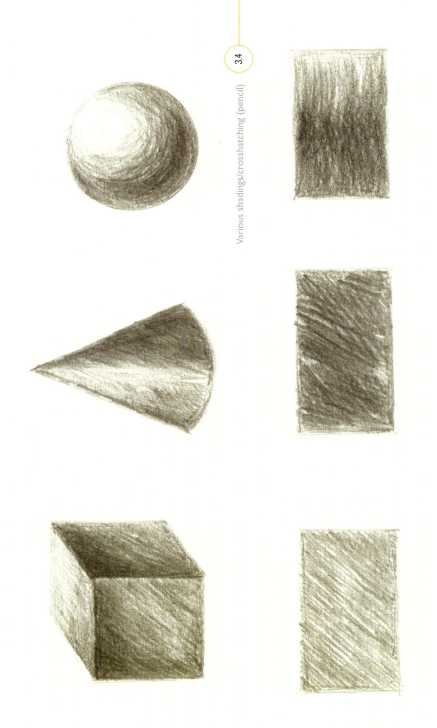

3.4

Various shadings/crosshatching (pencil)

Negative space drawing of a chair (pencil)

3.5

DEMONSTRATION: NEGATIVE SPACE

The way an experienced artist sees an object is different from the view of the person who has never drawn. The following negative space drawing demonstration will walk you through the steps on how to draw a space instead of the object.

NEGATIVE SPACE DRAWING DEMONSTRATION

1. Find two similar chairs that have several openings between different parts of the chair. Set one chair facing you. Turn the other chair 90 degrees (Figure 3.5).

2. Use your sketchbook and pencil.

3. Relax your right hand (or left hand if you are left-handed). Look at the chairs and try to trace the edges of the empty spaces.

4. Forget the details of each object, such as the cushion, arms, legs, and so on. Draw what you see as your eyes track the direction of the edge of the empty spaces. When the edge changes the direction, change the direction of your pencil.

5. Move your pencil slowly. Observe the changes in the empty spaces and record these changes on paper.

6. Add 45-degree angled pencil strokes to create shading in the negative spaces. This will create the contrast between the object and the background. The background makes the object stands out.

7. You can add a second layer of shading to make your background darker. Use a sharp pencil and trace the edges to make the object clean and crisp.

This is a simple demonstration. You also can stack one chair on top of the other one. Turn the top chair upside down. It will make the drawing a little harder.

EXERCISE 3.1

NEGATIVE SPACE

The negative space concept has been used in furniture design as well. Figure 3.6a shows a chair designed by Eric MacDonald, the winner the 2008 Wilsonart student design scholarship competition at the International Contemporary Furniture Design Fair, and Figure 3.6b shows a drawing of the chair using a negative space concept. Find another type of chair at your school or at another site, or use the example in Figure 3.6a to complete the following exercise.

1. Use your sketchbook and a pencil.

2. Relax your right hand (or left hand if you are left-handed). Look at the chair and pay attention to the composition. Try to trace the edges of the empty spaces.

3. Remember not to get caught up in details and parts of the chair, like the side red board and white legs in Figure 3.6a. Just record what you see; your eye should track the direction of the edge of the empty spaces. When the edge changes the direction, so should your pencil.

4. Move your pencil slowly. Observe the changes on the empty spaces and record these changes on paper.

5. Use 45-degree angled pencil strokes to add shadings in the negative spaces. It creates the contrast between the object and the background. The background makes the object stand out.

6. You also can change the direction of your shading in order to have some variation in the strokes. This can be achieved by multiple layers of shading, meaning you can shade an area a second or third time. Multiple layers of shading are important for negative space drawings.

Wilsonart chair (Photo courtesy of Macdonald, Wilsonart International)

Negative space drawing of Wilsonart chair (pencil)

3.6a

3.6b

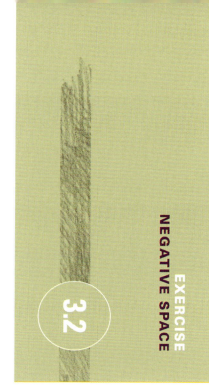

EXERCISE

NEGATIVE SPACE

3.2

This exercise uses an architectural design of a sustainable private residence in Mexico City. Figure 3.7a is a photo of the house and surrounding landscape, and Figure 3.7b is a drawing of it using the negative space concept.

1. Use your sketchbook and pencil.

2. Relax your right hand (or left hand if you are left-handed). Look at the building and pay attention to the composition. Try to trace the edges of the empty spaces.

3. Again, block out details, like windows and doors in this case. Just record what you see, and let your eye track the direction of the edges of the empty spaces. When the edge changes the direction, so should your pencil.

4. Move your pencil slowly. Observe the changes in the empty spaces and record these changes on paper.

5. You also can add some tree trunks in the background. Do this by perceiving the empty spaces between tree trunks and branches.

6. Use 45-degree angled pencil strokes to add shadings in the negative spaces. It creates the contrast between the object and the background. The background makes the object stand out.

7. Again, you also can change the direction of your shading in order to create variation in the strokes. This can be achieved by multiple layers of shading, a second or third time.

3.7a

Private residence in Mexico City (Photo courtesy of Santamarina Sustainable Residence project by PAUL CREMOUX studio)

Negative space drawing of residence in Mexico City (pencil)

3.7b

In order to become proficient with drawing using a negative space concept, practice with as many objects as you can find in everyday environments, like plants, flowers, vases, and furniture. Figures 3.8, 3.9, and 3.10 show some examples. Figure 3.8 is a negative space drawing of a chair. Figure 3.9 is a negative space drawing of the Kew House located in Melbourne, Australia. The three forms are suspended with a supporting structure of circular two-toned columns. Beneath the platform level is a big open space. Figure 3.10 is a negative space drawing of a staircase and hand railing.

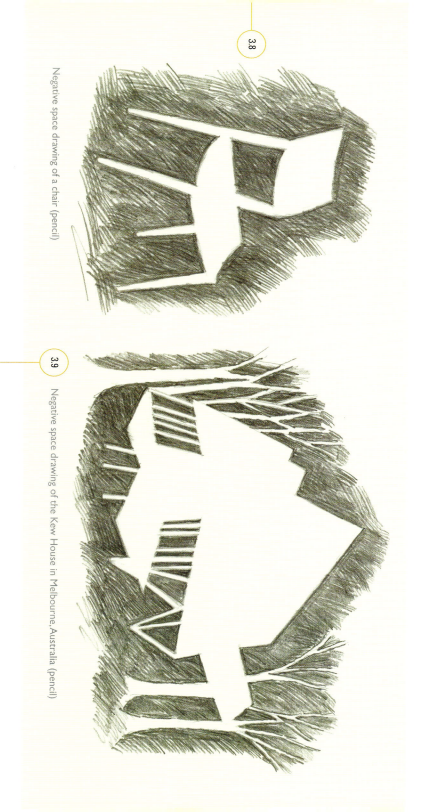

3.8

Negative space drawing of a chair (pencil)

3.9

Negative space drawing of the Kew House in Melbourne, Australia (pencil)

TIPS AND HINTS

- Be loose and relaxed while drawing.

- Perceive the spaces of objects (empty areas) and forget the details and names of the parts of the objects.

- Trace the edges of the empty areas.

- Add toned backgrounds to the drawings.

- Draw the toned background in different values (darkness and brightness) by using multiple layers of strokes.

- Use sharp pencil to make the edges clean and crisp.

3.10 Negative space drawing of a staircase and hand railing

SUMMARY

This chapter introduced the concept of negative space and positive form. Space perception is the second drawing skill that you have to master. After you finish this chapter, you are able to:

- Understand the concept of negative space.

- Understand why negative space drawings match right-side brain thinking.

- Perceive negative spaces.

- Understand the concept of composition in drawing.

- Use a viewfinder.

- Explore basic shading/stroke skills for toned backgrounds.

- See objects in spaces without reference to preexisting memories of their shapes.

- Use the right side of your brain to draw!

KEY TERMS

Balance	Detail	Negative Space	Shading/Strokes
Composition	Focal Point	Positive Form	Viewfinder

ADDITIONAL EXERCISES

1. Choose a piece of furniture or interior object, such as chairs or vases with flowers, and create a negative space drawing.

2. Find a staircase with open railings. Draw the staircase railings with empty areas.

Reference

Edwards, Betty, *Drawing on the Right Side of the Brain*. New York; Jeremy P. Tarcher/Putnam, a member of Penguin Putnam, Inc., 1999.

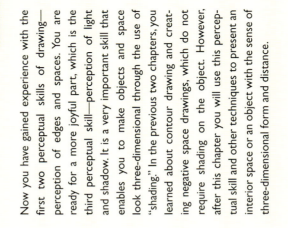

4

PERCEPTION OF LIGHT AND SHADOW

Now you have gained experience with the first two perceptual skills of drawing—perception of edges and spaces. You are ready for a more joyful part, which is the third perceptual skill—perception of light and shadow. It is a very important skill that enables you to make objects and space look three-dimensional through the use of "shading." In the previous two chapters, you learned about contour drawing and creating negative space drawings, which do not require shading on the object. However, after this chapter you will use this perceptual skill and other techniques to present an interior space or an object with the sense of three-dimensional form and distance.

OBSERVING VALUES

Value means darkness and brightness. When you observe and draw a building or space, you need to see differences in tones of light and dark on each wall, ceiling, or floor. Figure 4.1 shows a value bar going from pure white to pure black. Pale, light tones are called "high" in value, while dark tones are called "low" in value.

Value, Light, and Shadow

When you draw in pencil, you translate the colors of nature into black and white. It is just like you are taking a photo in black and white, and various shades of gray are visible. This conversion from color into different shades of gray is called value. Every color has a value. For example, red bricks are fairly dark, almost black except the highlighted areas (Figures 4.2 and 4.3), while wood siding is medium gray (Figure 4.4), and stuccos are very pale gray, almost white (Figure 4.5).

Value and shadow are used by the designer as the basis for making a rendering look realistic. Without value designation, a drawing does not have any depth or a sense of three-dimensional form or distance. Without the presence of light, shade, and shadow, objects would appear flat and uninteresting.

4.1 Value bar (pencil)

4.2 Brick chimney (pencil)

4.3 Window in brick wall (pencil)

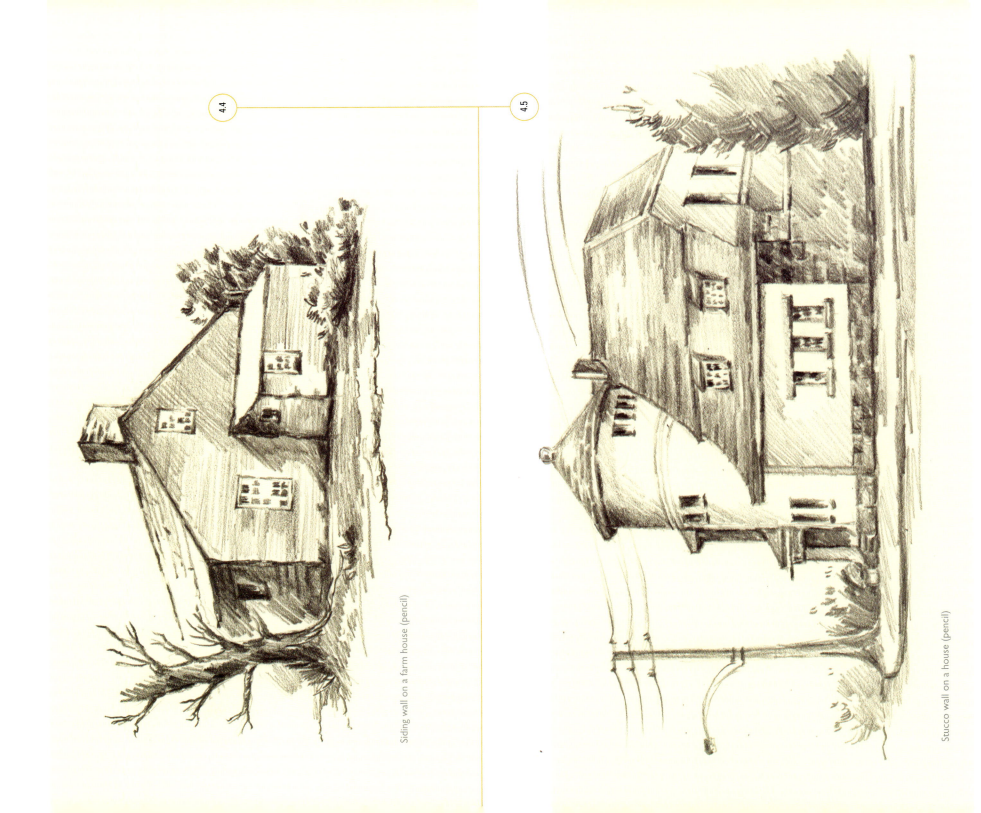

4.4

4.5

Siding wall on a farm house (pencil)

Stucco wall on a house (pencil)

Lights fall on all objects from one source or many sources. Light gives objects the definition of their shapes. You will always see the following phenomena about light, shade, and shadows:

Highlight: The brightest light, which appears where light from the source falls most directly on the object.

Cast shadow: The object blocks light rays, causing the darkest shadow.

Crest shadow: A shadow that is on the crest of a rounded form, between the highlight and the reflected light. Crest shadows and reflected lights are very difficult to distinguish at first. But the crest shadow is the key to round out the object in a three-dimensional form.

Reflected light: Light will be reflected back onto the object from the surface around the object.

Those surfaces of the object not receiving direct light rays will be in shade. Usually there is reflected light on a shaded surface.

When you sketch an interior space, you will always see reflections, especially on shaded surfaces. Also, you will always see cast shadows, such as those underneath a piece of furniture. Sometimes you will see highlights because of a lighting source nearby. Figure 4.6 is an interior sketch in which you can see cast shadows at the entrance and on the wall, reflections on the shade surface, and some highlights on the wall.

4.6   A staircase in a hotel interior space (pencil)

Drawing Shadows

As described in previous chapters, the left side of the brain will not pay attention to negative space or upside-down information. Research on the human brain indicates that the right side of the brain is not only able to perceive the shapes of particular shadows, but also specializes in deriving meaning from patterns or shadows (Edwards, 2002, p. 197). Therefore, if you draw the shapes of lighted areas and shadowed areas just as you perceive them, the viewer will not notice those shapes. Instead, the viewer will see "real" objects and feel them to be three-dimensional.

Based on this theory, it is not necessary to outline the object that is under a light source. All you need to do is draw the shape of the shadow. The right side of the brain is able to extrapolate from this incomplete information and envision a complete image. Figure 4.7 is a drawing of a Corinthian capital and statue, completed with just shadows. It looks real even though some pieces of it are missing in the shadow area. However, the right side of your brain is able to complete the image.

As introduced in Chapter 3, perceiving negative space is the second important drawing skill. Just like drawing by shadows, you can just draw the negative spaces with shadings. Figure 4.8 is an example of an interior space with staircase. The railings at the staircase were drawn by perceiving negative space by perceiving negative space with shading. You do not need to really draw each single railing. Instead, you just need to fill in the negative space with shadings. It is important to show a variety of values in the shading even though they may cover very small areas.

4.6   Drawing shadows of a Corinthian capital and a statue

Shading or Crosshatching

Crosshatching is a fundamental technique in sketching. The ability to crosshatch is a mark of a trained designer. Crosshatching presents the designer's personal style of drawing. You will develop your own style as you become more comfortable and mature with freehand sketching skills.

Figure 4.9 shows typical crosshatching that is used often in pencil drawings. Showing the pencil strokes on the drawing and not smearing them adds a certain signature to a designer's drawing style.

Pencil strokes and crosshatching (pencil)

The following is a basic procedure of crosshatching:

1. Hold your pencil firmly and make a group of parallel strokes, as in Figure 4.9. Place your pencil down firmly on the paper. Your wrist remains stationary and your fingers pull the pencil back just for each successive stroke.

2. Practice making sets of strokes until you find the direction, spacing, and length of strokes that seem right for you.

3. The next step is to make crosshatching. The cross set is made at an angle only slightly different from the original set, as in the background of Figure 4.9.

4. By changing the angle of crossing, a different style of crosshatch is achieved. Figure 4.9 presents several different crosshatchings: full cross (strokes crossing at different angles); cross-contour (usually curved strokes); hooked-hatching (usually the strokes all look like a hook at the end). The last two crosshatching styles are used for a curved surface.

PROCEDURE OF CROSSHATCHING

Before you start to draw an object or advance to the next interior perspective drawing, it is very important to learn how to do shading or crosshatching. Both shading and crosshatching are technical terms for creating a variety of tones or values in a drawing. Shading or crosshatching means laying down sets of pencil strokes, and often crossing the strokes at angles. Figures 4.10 and 4.11 are examples of drawing entirely with crosshatching. Figure 4.10 presents two simple geometric forms that are drawn by using crosshatching. You can see crest shadow on the sphere, which is between the highlight and the reflected light. Figure 4.11 shows a Corinthian column. The background in Figure 4.11 is created by crosshatching. You also can see the crosshatching technique in all the pencil drawings in this chapter.

Forms Defined by Surfaces

One of the important techniques of drawing with a variety of values is to use surfaces to define the object instead of using lines. The outlines of the object need to be blended in with the tonal of value on the surface. You will not see any outlines when the drawing is completed. Figure 4.12 shows an example of the technique of using surfaces to define forms. You also can see this technique used in other drawings in this chapter.

Leaving White on the Paper

Leaving white on the paper is another technique when you use crosshatching, especially in the areas with reflections. Leaving white on the paper makes your drawing look more alive. The white areas usually would be in the area with highlight or reflection. For example, Figure 4.13 is an atrium in a hotel lobby. By leaving some of the areas white, brightness is added to the space to simulate sunlight coming through windows. Reflections are added to the dark openings on the wall.

Cylinder and sphere (pencil)

4.10

4.11

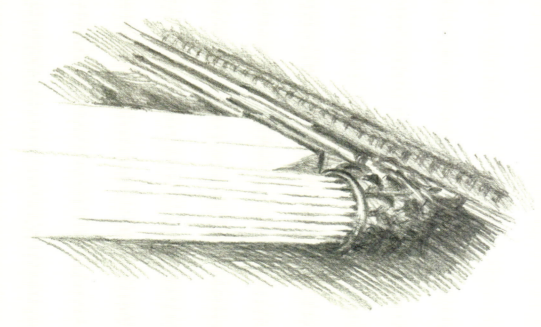

Corinthian column (pencil)

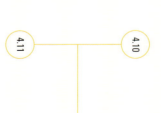

4.12 An open two-story entrance (pencil)

DEMONSTRATION: SEEING LIGHT AND SHADOW

The purpose of the following simple demonstrations is to introduce the concepts of value, light, shading, and crosshatching.

Creating Contrast on an Object

Creating contrast on a main object is very important to show the sense of depth and three-dimensional form. Creating contrast means to show different values on two surfaces using values that are not close on the value bar. Strong contrast means two values that are farther apart on the value bar. Soft contrast means two values that are closer on the value bar. Typically, strong contrast is created on the main object that is the focal point in the drawing, while soft contrast is created either in the background or on the object that will not draw viewer's attention. You still do not want to use lines to define the object, as discussed earlier. What you need to do is put the emphasis along the edge of two surfaces and increase the value contrast, although there might be reflections in the dark shade surface. If there is no contrast of values in the drawing—in other words, if the values are the same or very close in the entire drawing—then the space or object looks flat and lacks a sense of three-dimensional form and depth. All examples of the interior sketches in this chapter present the technique of creating contrast on main objects.

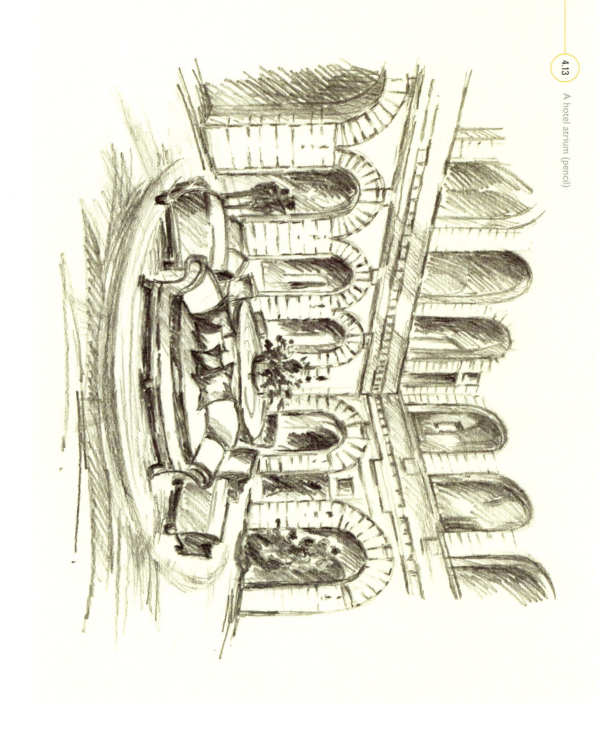

4.13   A hotel atrium (pencil)

VALUE DEMONSTRATION #1 — CUBE IN SPACE

1. Use the cube as an example.

2. Use pencil to draw an isometric view of the cube. (An isometric view is different from a view incorporating perspective. There is no vanishing point in an isometric view. Lines are parallel.)

3. Define the direction of the lighting source.

4. Analyze three different values on the cube and the direction of the lighting source.

5. Use pencil to start shading on the lightest surface of the cube.

6. It is important to change the value even though you are shading the same surface.

7. After you finish shading, you will be surprised to see that the cube becomes a solid, three-dimensional object (Figure 4.14).

4.14

Cube in space using different values

VALUE DEMONSTRATION #2 –
CLASSICAL COLUMNS IN THE PANTHEON

This demonstration provides an example of using surfaces to define forms instead of using outlines. Figure 4.15 is a black-and-white photo that shows architectural classical columns in the Pantheon in Rome

1. It is important to keep in mind that this demonstration emphasizes using the surface to present the object, which means the outlines need to be blended into the shading.

2. Using pencil to draw columns with lines is a bad practice. The drawing looks flat and lacks of sense of three-dimensional form because there is no tonal value in the drawing.

3. Use pencil to sketch the outline of the columns. It is a very simple perspective and not hard to sketch.

4. Draw the columns with shading. Start with lighter shading first. Use surface to define the features on the column and use different values to present different surfaces (Figure 4.16).

5. Use crosshatching for shading.

6. Do not try to make certain areas too dark at first. It is better to finish all the shadings with a variety of tonal values. Then come back to put emphasis on the main object.

Corinthian column in the Pantheon in Rome (Photo © Adrian Mars)

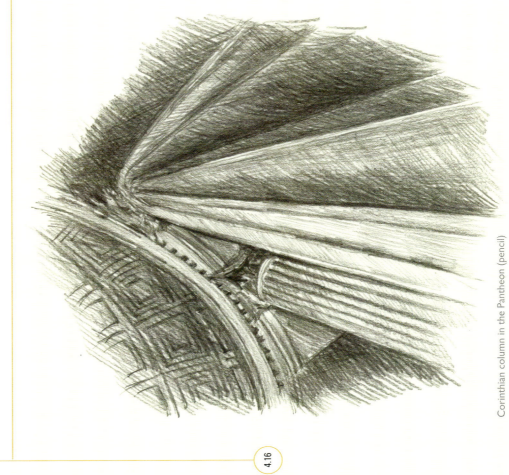

Corinthian column in the Pantheon (pencil)

EXERCISE
PLASTER VASE

4.1

Use a plaster vase as an object to draw. Set up the plaster vase on a table in your work space. Review the concept of composition and use a viewfinder to define the object. Use a pencil to draw the outlines of the vase. Make sure that the perspective is accurate. Use shading or crosshatching to show different values on the drawing. It is critical to pay attention to value changes in the shadow area. Figure 4.17 shows an example of a plaster vase drawing to follow using this technique.

EXERCISE
PRACTICING USING SURFACES TO
DEFINE FORMS

4.2

This exercise will help you to practice how to apply the technique of using surfaces to define forms in your drawing. Use the Ionic column shown in Figure 4.18 as your model. Draw it in you sketchbook with pencil. Do not use outlines to define the column. Use shadings with a variety of values to define the object in order to present the sense of three-dimensional form.

4.17

Plaster vase (pencil)

4.18

Ionic column (Photo© Donald Weeks)

INTERIOR PERSPECTIVE—KNOWING MORE ABOUT VALUE AND SHADOW

This exercise will help you to get familiar with shading to present a variety of values in drawing. Use pencil to draw in your sketchbook the interior perspective shown in Figure 4.19. Make sure the perspective is accurate before you start shading.

While creating this drawing, pay attention to reflections on shaded surfaces, the cast shadow underneath the sofa, and leaving white on the windows and sofa, as well as the variety of values on the drapery.

4.19

Residential interior space (pencil)

- It is important to show value changes in the shadow area. This value change is caused by reflections from the environment. Otherwise, your drawings will look lifeless.

- You can use lines to start your drawing. However, you will have to blend outlines with your shadings so that you will not see the outlines after you complete your drawings. Do not use lines to define the edges.

- Build your tones gradually; try not to get too dark too fast, especially when you are working with pencil.

- It is important to create strong contrast at your focal point. You also need to put emphasis on the transition edges.

4. PERCEPTION OF LIGHT AND SHADOW   71

SUMMARY

In this chapter, you:

- Were introduced to the fourth perception skill—how to perceive light and shadow.

- Learned basic concept of value, shading, and crosshatching.

- Learned the concepts of cast shadow, crest shadow, highlight, and reflection in interior environments.

- Practiced how to draw a cube or plaster vase with shading and crosshatching to show different values.

- Learned drawing techniques, including drawing by shadows; shading or crosshatching; forms defined by surfaces; leaving white on the paper; and creating contrast on an object.

- Had the chance to practice interior perspectives both from a photo and a drawing.

In order to make your main object stand out as a focal point, you need to create strong contrast on that object. You also need to show value changes on the same surface because of the reflections from the environment.

KEY TERMS

Brightness	Crest Shadow	Highlight	Shadow
Cast Shadow	Crosshatching	Reflection	Texture
Contrast	Darkness	Shading	Value

1. Use a plaster vase or other plaster geometric shapes—cube, cylinder, or sphere—as objects. You can group two or three plaster objects together. Set up appropriate lighting. Use shading and crosshatching to draw objects. Observe objects carefully and pay attention to different values.

2. Choose your favorite interior design color photos. You can download photos from the Internet or get photos from magazines. Draw the interior space in the photo with a pencil. Convert the colors from the photo into different values.

3. Choose drawings in this chapter. Draw them in your sketchbook to practice how to leave white on paper, how to draw shadows, how to define the surfaces of object, and how to create contrast on objects.

4. If you are comfortable with perspective at this point, you also can go to your favorite interior space to sketch. Pay special attention to the perspective in the space you are drawing. It is important to create contrast for values on the objects that are your focal point.

Reference

Edwards, Betty, *Drawing on the Right Side of the Brain*. New York: Jeremy P. Tarcher/Putnam, a member of Penguin Putnam, Inc., 1999.

5

PERCEPTION OF SPATIAL RELATIONSHIPS

The fourth drawing skill is how to perceive spatial relationships, which means how to see the object or space and draw it in perspective with correct proportions. You may say, "It is too hard to draw it in correct perspective." It is true that perspective is not very easy to master in drawing, especially for beginners. Why does the perception-of-spatial-relationships skill seem so difficult? The reason is that there are two subsets of skills involved. The first skill is seeing angles relative to the vertical and horizontal planes in the space, which is also called perspective, and the second skill is seeing proportions relative to each other in the space. If you understand these two concepts and see an object or space in a correct perspective with correct proportion, you will be able to draw with correct perspective.

ARCHITECTURAL PERSPECTIVES

There are many different ways to lay out your perspectives, such as the freehand or estimated method, and the common method. The freehand method is quick and

does not need floor plans, elevations, and sections of the space. The common method is more accurate because a floor plan and perspective:

either a section or elevation drawing are required. Since the subject focus here is freehand drawing, the freehand method of constructing an interior perspective will be introduced and described. Instead of introducing all the technical terminology of perspective, a visual guide with simple basic terminology is provided in this chapter. You can use the right side of your brain to visualize the concept. It will help you to understand all different perspectives.

Perspective is very important in interior sketching and architectural rendering. But do not be intimidated by its complexity. As long as you understand the concepts and know the rules, you will be able to master this skill after practice. There are three different perspectives: one-point perspective, two-point perspective, and three-point perspective.

There are several terms and concepts that are fundamental to further understanding perspective:

Horizon Line (H.L.): The line where the viewer's eye is located. The horizon line represents the eye level of the viewer. If the viewer is standing, the horizon line will be 5 to 6 feet above the ground line.

Vanishing Point (V.P.): The point on the horizon line at which parallel lines converge. One-point perspectives have one vanishing point. Two-point perspectives have two vanishing points, and three-point perspectives have three vanishing points.

Picture Plane (P.P.): An imaginary transparent "window" in which the perspective view is drawn. In most perspectives the picture plane is positioned between the viewer and the object or the space that is drawn.

Ground Line (G. L.): The meeting place of picture plane and the ground.

Cone of Vision (C.V.): The cone of vision represents what a viewer will see within a perspective drawing. Items located outside the cone of vision tend to appear distorted. This cone is drawn on the floor plan as a 60-degree triangle.

Different Views

Differences in the location and height of the viewer will yield different perspectives. If the viewer is parallel to the object or the viewing plane is perpendicular to the picture plane, then it is one-point perspective, such as Figures 5.1 and 5.2. If the viewer is at an angle to the object, then it will be two-point perspective, as shown in Figures 5.3 and 5.4. If the object is a skyscraper or a multistory hotel atrium, then the viewer will have three-point perspective, like Figures 5.5 and 5.6. The height

One-point perspective of an interior space (marker, ink, colored pencil)

Two-point perspective of an interior space (marker, ink, colored pencil)

Two-point perspective of an interior space (marker, ink, colored pencil)

5.4

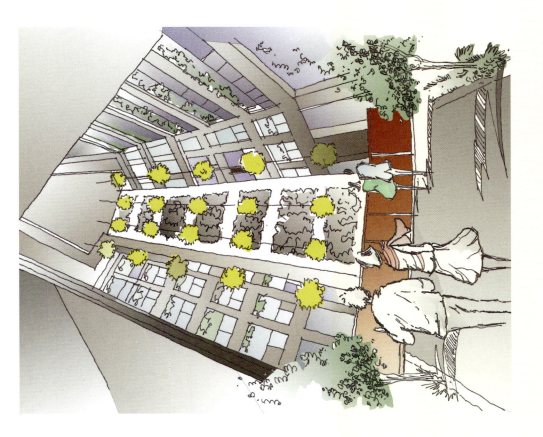

5.5

Three-point perspective of
an interior space (marker, ink,
Photoshop)

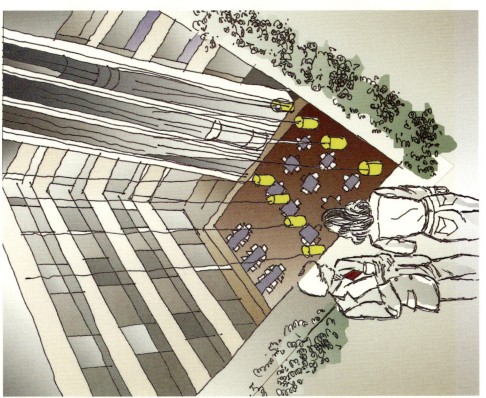

5.6

Three-point perspective of
an interior space (marker, ink,
Photoshop)

5.7 Worm's-eye view of a hotel atrium (marker, ink, colored pencil)

of the viewer also will affect the perspec-tive. If you are lying down on the ground, you will have a worm's-eye view (Figure 5.7). If you are standing in front of the building or object, you will have an eye-level view. If you are in an airplane or on a taller building and

looking down to a lower building, then you will have bird's-eye view (Figure 5.8).

Figures 5.5 and 5.6 are freehand draw-ings that have been edited by Photoshop. Detailed procedures for transforming free-hand drawing to digital drawing are provided in Chapter 10.

Bird's-eye view of a hotel courtyard (marker, ink, colored pencil)

5.8

One-Point Perspective

In one-point perspective, the viewer is parallel to the space in front of him or her. The front and back elevations of a space or object are parallel to the picture plane and are drawn as true elevations. In one-point perspective, there is one vanishing point located on the horizon line. All lines in the drawing, including perspective lines, converge to a single vanishing point. Perspective lines define the sides of the object and converge at the single vanishing point. Objects located outside of the cone of vision tend to appear distorted. There are many examples in the space around you. Keep your eyes open and look for examples of one-point perspective. Try to determine where the vanishing point and the horizon line are in the examples. Figure 5.9 shows a typical one-point perspective with horizon line and vanishing point.

Two-Point Perspective: Adding More Dimension to Your Space

While one-point perspective is most often used by artists and designers throughout history, it is common for designers to view reality in two-point perspective. In two-point perspective, the viewer is at an angle to the building or space in front of him or her. There are two vanishing points located on the horizon line, in which all lines of a building or space converge. All lines in two-point perspectives are either vertical lines or perspective lines. The horizontal edges of a space converge to two vanishing points as perspective lines; the vertical edges of a space remain vertical. Two-point perspective drawings have true vertical lines as well as perspective (depth) lines. Objects located outside of the cone of vision tend to appear distorted. In perspective drawings, objects appear to diminish in size as they recede from the viewer. Figure 5.10 shows a typical two-point perspective with horizon line and vanishing points.

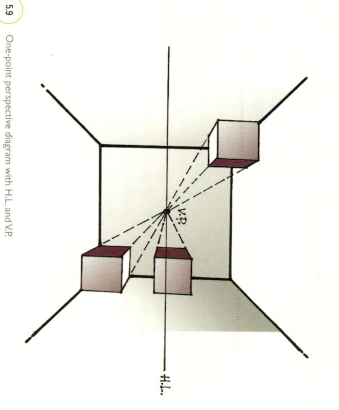

5.9

One-point perspective diagram with H.L. and V.P.

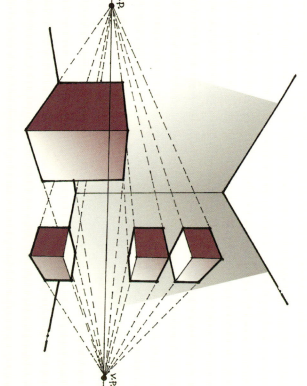

5.10

Two-point perspective diagram with H.L. and V.P.s

Three-Point Perspective: Adding More Dimension to Your World

There are some instances where three-point perspective can occur, such as when you are inside a hotel atrium and looking up, or when you are inside a multistory hotel building looking down the interior atrium. In the first case, both sides of the building are visible, just like in two-point perspective; the third vanishing point occurs as the vertical lines of the building converge up in the sky (Figure 5.11a). When looking down from a tall building, the vanishing point occurs below the ground line (Figure 5.11b). In three-point perspective, all edges are oblique to the picture plane and all lines are perspective lines. Perspective lines converge to three vanishing points, two located on the horizon line and one usually above or below the horizon line. Objects located outside the cone of vision tend to appear distorted. Objects appear to diminish in size as they recede from the viewer.

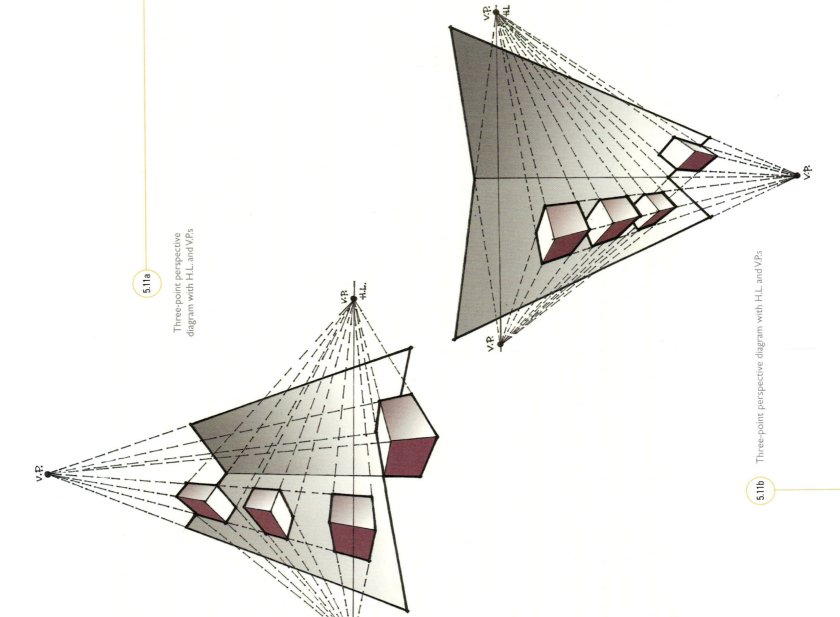

5.11a

Three-point perspective diagram with H.L. and V.P.s

5.11b

Three-point perspective diagram with H.L. and V.P.s

PROPORTION

Proportion is as important as perspective in drawing. As previously mentioned, the second and subset of skills involved in the perception of spatial relationships is drawing the space or object with correct proportion. Proportion means the ratio of width and height—for example, the window is twice as tall as it is wide. The ratio is 1:2. Therefore, you will need to draw the window height twice as long as its width in order to present the correct proportion. In mathematics, ratios are expressed as numbers, such as 1:3, which means one of this to three of that. Ratios seem like a left side of the brain concept because they are expressed in numbers.

But in drawing, ratios become an easy way to assess proportional relationships among the parts of a composition. Normally, something is chosen to be "one," the basic unit, and that unit is rationalized or proportionalized with all other parts. When you draw the width, call it "one." Then measure off the basic units and count it off "one to two." The ratio is 1:2. It is an easy way to measure the proportion and transfer it into a drawing.

Pencil: Visual Measuring Device

Visual measuring can be used to determine the relationship of lengths and widths of forms. When drawing an interior space viewed from an oblique angle, for example, you need first to determine the angles of the edges relative to the horizontal and vertical by using a visual measuring device—the pencil.

Your pencil is very convenient! Line it up with an angle that you want to draw on paper, then move the pencil to your sketchbook to "see" the angle where it will be drawn. (Figure 5.12).

You may use your pencil to find comparative measurements too. Hold your pencil as shown (Figure 5.13), then stretch your arm or lock your elbow against anything you want to measure. Of course this does not need to be exact. Compare A to B—it is roughly half. Therefore, draw it that way and your subject will have the correct proportion.

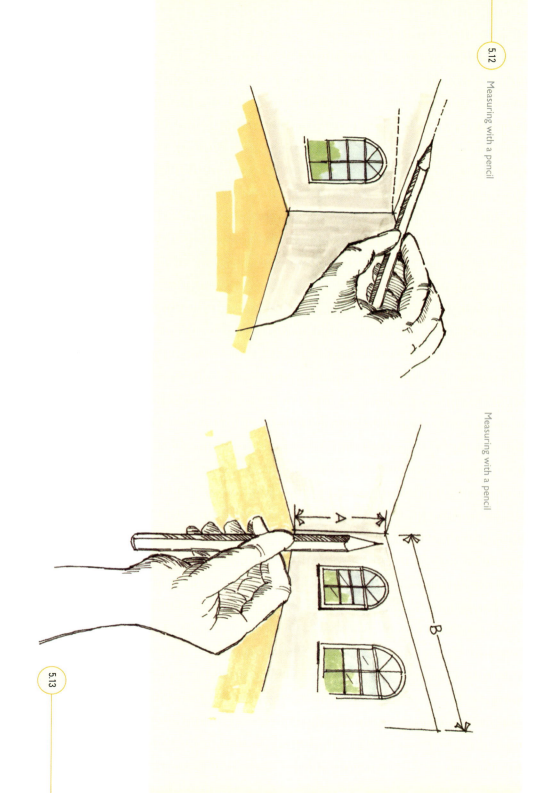

5.12

Measuring with a pencil

5.13

Measuring with a pencil

Here are some key principles and measuring methods of perspective, along with a visual guide:

1. Parallel lines (such as the edges of cabinets in Figure 5.14) converge into vanishing points on a horizon line for the plane in which they lie.

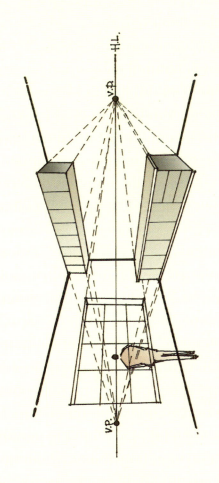

5.14

Visual guide of principles of perspective

2. Vanishing points for the perspectives of a rectangular object or space are the intersections of the perspective lines for the horizontal planes and perspective lines for the vertical planes (Figure 5.15).

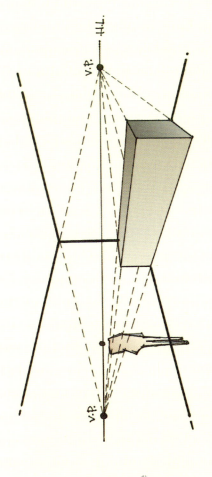

5.15

Visual guide of principles of perspective

continued from previous page

3. Objects appear to diminish in size as they recede from the viewer (Figure 5.16).

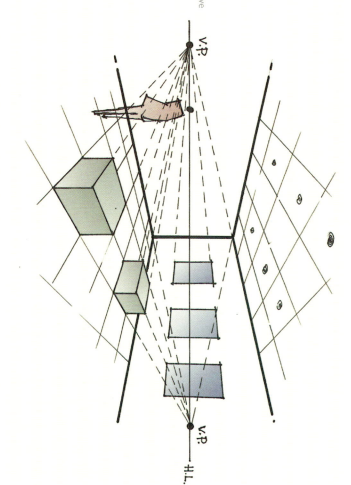

4. A rectangular object can be divided into equal parts by first locating the center. The center can be located by drawing two diagonal lines to connect the opposite corners of a rectangular. The center point and centerline are at the intersection of the two diagonal lines. Then subdivide the face of the object with additional diagonals to divide each half into two more sections (Figure 5.17).

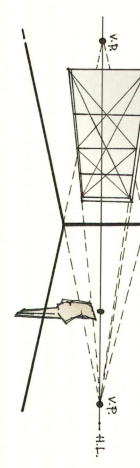

5. When circles are oblique to the picture plane, they are drawn as an ellipse. To draw a circle, first draw a square plane and then subdivide the plane with diagonals to locate the centerline of the object. To locate the ellipse within the square, intermediate points are needed; find them by dividing each half of the diagonal line into thirds. The circle intersects the point that is one-third away from the corner (Figure 5.18).

5.18

Visual guide of principles of perspective

DEMONSTRATION: INTERIOR PERSPECTIVE

The purpose of doing the following simple demonstration is to become familiar with the concepts and terminology of perspective.

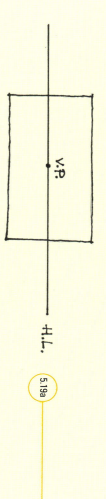

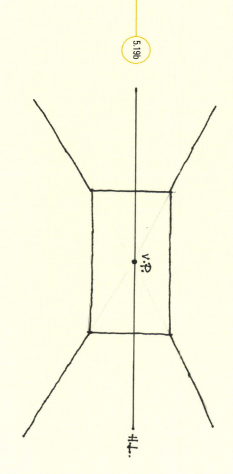

One-point perspective demonstration: a. horizon line and back wall; b. horizon line, back wall, and side walls

1. Use your classroom as an example and draw a one-point perspective of the room.

2. Before starting the demonstration, review the concepts of one-point perspective, horizon line or eye line, and vanishing point.

3. Identify the horizon line, or eye line, and start with the horizon line first.

4. Identify the vanishing point.

5. Use your pencil to measure the proportion of the back wall and draw the back wall first (Figure 5.19a).

6. Then connect the vanishing point and each corner of the back wall and extend the lines (Figure 5.19b).

7. You will have both side walls (extended lines).

8. Identify the location of the picture frames on the left side of the wall.

9. Connect both the top and bottom points of the picture frame with the vanishing point.

10. Use your judgment to determine the width of each of the picture frames. Make sure the proportion of the picture frame is correct. Keep in mind that the width of the frame becomes narrower as it is located farther away from the viewer (Figure 5.20a).

11. Identify the location of the bookcase on the left side of the wall.

12. Connect both the top and bottom points of the bookcase with the vanishing point.

13. Use your pencil to measure the width of the bookcase. Make sure to show the thickness of the board used for the bookcase (Figure 5.20a).

14. You also can show some books in the bookcase.

15. Identify the location of the window on the right side of the wall (Figure 20b).

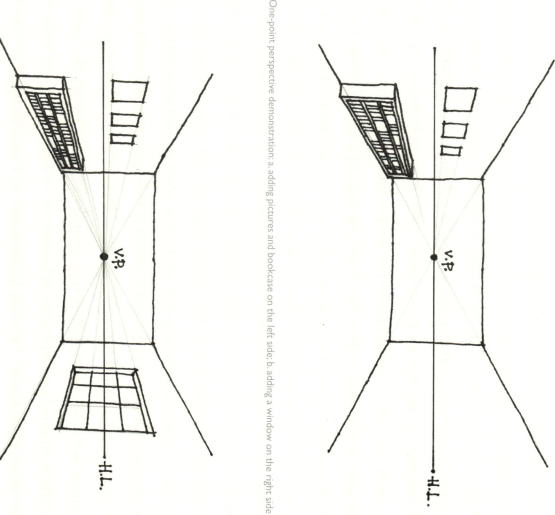

One-point perspective demonstration: a. adding pictures and bookcase on the left side; b. adding a window on the right side wall

5.20b

5.20a

continued from previous page

16. Connect both the top and bottom points of the window with the vanishing point.

17. Pay attention to the window thickness. Do not forget to use double lines to show that the window is recessed within the wall. Connect horizontal window grids with the vanishing point.

18. The vertical window grids remain vertical, but the spacing appears smaller the farther away the window grids are from the viewer (Figure 5.20b).

19. Draw horizontal lines as ceiling grids. The spacing appears smaller the farther away the ceiling grids are from the viewer.

20. Measure an equal portion on top of the back wall with dividing marks.

21. Connect the vanishing point with all dividing marks and extend these lines. They further subdivide the ceiling grids to form acoustic ceiling tiles.

22. Draw can lights on the ceiling. The ones that are close to the viewer appear larger.

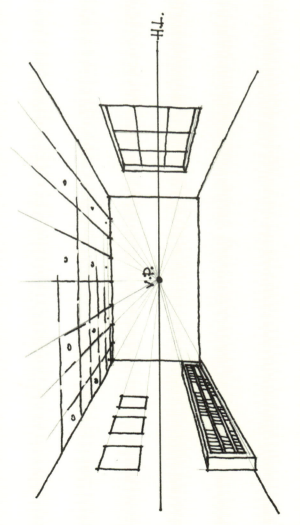

5.21 One-point perspective demonstration: adding ceiling grids

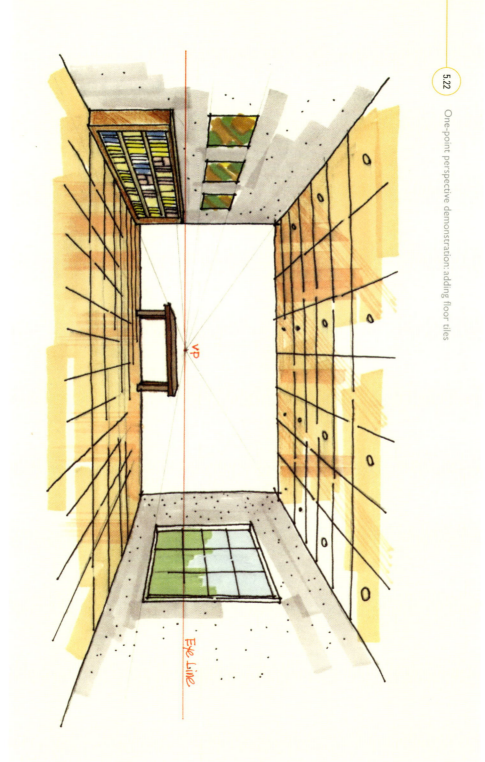

5.22

One-point perspective demonstration: adding floor tiles

continued from previous page

23. Draw horizontal lines as floor tiles. The spacing appears smaller the farther away the lines are from the viewer.

24. Measure an equal portion on bottom of the back wall with dividing marks as the measurement of each floor tile.

25. Connect the vanishing point with all dividing marks and extend these lines. They are the floor tiles.

26. Remember that all parallel lines of objects in the real world will converge to the vanishing point.

27. Pay special attention to windows, ceiling grids, and floor tiles because these are the most challenging elements for beginners.

28. Figure 5.22 shows a completed interior one-point perspective.

1. Find an interior setting on campus, such as a lounge in a student union or a building lobby.

2. Review the concepts of two-point perspective, such as horizon line, vanishing point, and perspective lines.

3. Choose your position, at an angle to two walls.

4. Identify the horizon line, or eye line, and start with the eye line first.

5. Identify the vanishing points.

6. Use your pencil to measure the proportion of the space and the object.

7. Remember that all parallel lines of objects in the real world will converge at the vanishing point.

8. Pay special attention to windows, ceiling grids, and floor tiles because these are the most challenging elements for beginners.

9. Figure 5.23 shows a completed interior two-point perspective. The second vanishing point is off the page. You have to use your imagination to know that it is there.

Two-point perspective demonstration with horizon line and vanish points

5.23

Getting familiar with perspective is important. The more practice you have the better you will be at it. Find photos that display one-point perspective, two-point perspective, and three-point perspective. Analyze each photo by identifying horizon line (eye line) and vanishing points, as well as perspective lines. Use a red pen to draw the horizon line and vanishing points on each photo.

EXERCISE

GETTING FAMILIAR WITH PERSPECTIVE

5.1

EXERCISE

PERSPECTIVE PRACTICE— CUBES IN SPACE

5.2

This exercise will help you to practice one-point perspective, two-point perspective, and three-point perspective, so that you will gain a more complete understanding of the concepts. Draw the cubes shown in Figures 5.24, 5.25 5.26 and 5.27 in your sketchbook. You can use a pencil to complete the shading. These cubes are drawn with different horizon lines or eye levels, and the cubes are arranged at different angles to each other.

Use your straight-edge or triangle to construct a perspective diagram for each of the sketches, similar to those shown in Figures 5.28, 5.29, 5.30, and 5.31. In your perspective diagram, you need to identify the horizon line and vanishing points.

After you complete this exercise and your eyes become more trained in seeing perspective, you will be on your way to using direct observation to accurately draw any object or space in correct perspective.

5.24 Perspective exercise—two cubes in space

5.25 Perspective exercise—two cubes in space

Perspective exercise—two cubes in space

Perspective exercise—two cubes in space

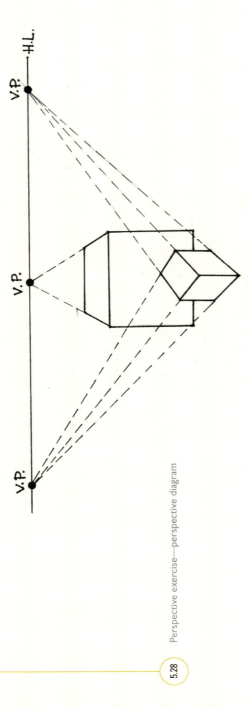

V.P. — H.L.

V.P.

V.P.

5.28

Perspective exercise—perspective diagram

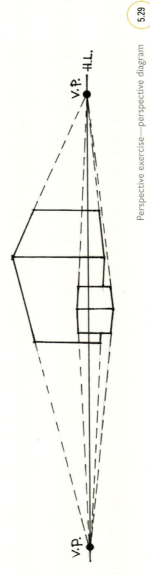

V.P. — H.L.

V.P.

5.29

Perspective exercise—perspective diagram

V.P.

V.P.

V.P.

H.L.

Perspective exercise—perspective diagram

5.31

5.30

Perspective exercise—perspective diagram

V.P.

V.P.

V.P.

V.P.

H.L.

TIPS AND HINTS

- A general rule of thumb for perspective—the object will become smaller when it is farther away from the viewer. For example, the spacing of the lines forming a window grid or ceiling grid will become closer when the grid is farther away from the viewer.

- Notice that the shadow that is cast by the sun or artificial lighting also converges toward the vanishing point.

- If the vanishing point is too far away to locate, you will have to use your judgment to find an imaginary vanishing point.

- When you choose your location for sketching, try not to get too close to the object.

- Build your tones gradually. Try not to get too dark too fast, especially when you are working with pencil. Otherwise, you may find it difficult to lighten an area or erase it.

SUMMARY

In this chapter, you:

- Were introduced to the fourth perception skill—how to perceive spatial relationships, which involves learning about perspective and proportion.

- Learned basic terminologies, such as horizon line, vanishing point, perspective lines, one-point perspective, two-point perspective, and three-point perspective, as well as bird's-eye's view and worm's-eye view.

- Practiced how to draw one-point, two-point, and three-point perspective.

The major difference between one-point and two-point perspective is that one-point perspective has one vanishing point, and two-point perspective has two vanishing points at different locations on the eye line, or horizon line. If you are standing parallel to one wall of the space, then your drawing will have a one-point perspective. If you are standing at an angle to two walls, then your sketch will have a two-point perspective. Three-point perspective has three vanishing points, two of which are located on the horizon line, while the third one is located either above or below the horizon line.

KEY TERMS

Bird's-Eye View	Ground Line	Picture Plane
Cone of Vision	Horizon Line	Proportion
Eye-Level View	One-Point Perspective	Three-Point Perspective
Eye Line	Perspective Lines	Two-Point Perspective
		Vanishing Point
		Worm's-Eye View

ADDITIONAL EXERCISES

1. Chose any drawing in this chapter and construct the perspective diagram in your sketchbook. Show the horizon line and vanishing points in your drawing.

2. Choose your favorite angle in your house or apartment; draw a one-point or two-point perspective. Remember to use your pencil as a visual measuring tool for angles.

3. Create a field sketch by choosing a location on campus. Sketch an interior space in one-point or two-point perspective.

4. Choose a location in a local shopping mall for a field sketch. Sketch the storefront in one-point or two-point perspective.

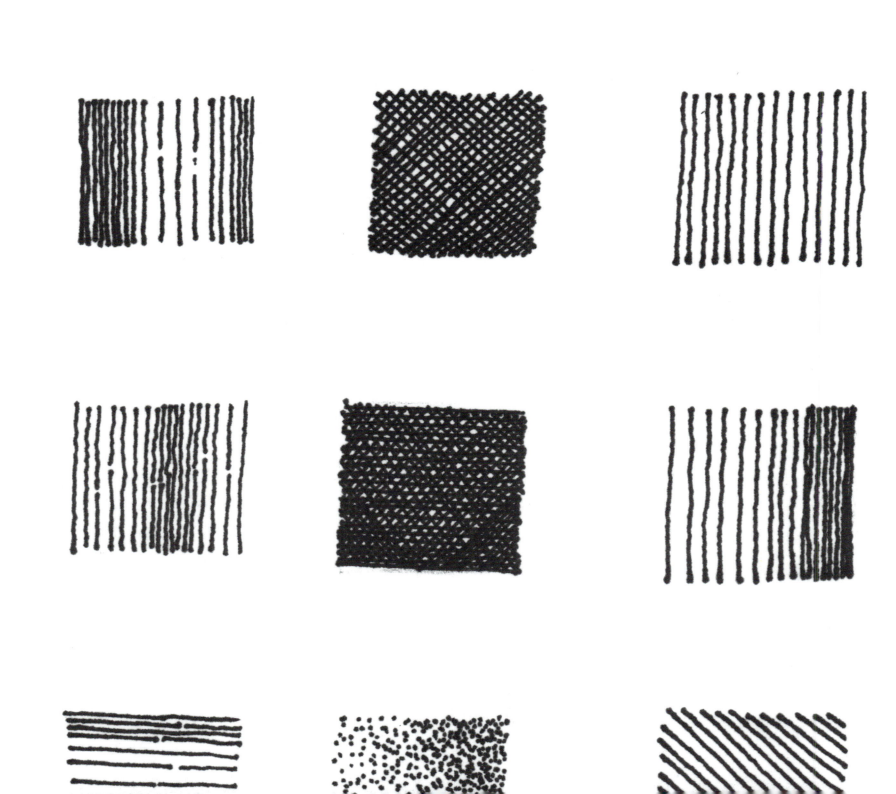

6

TEXTURE

Although you have learned how to draw an object or a setting with accurate perspective and appropriate values, it is very important to be able to master the skill of presenting texture for different materials is another important aspect. In this chapter, two different media, including pencil and ink (Sharpie), will be introduced. The technique of presenting texture or material plays a crucial role in the interior design sketching process.

PRESENTING TEXTURE WITH A PENCIL

The purpose of this simple demonstration is to introduce the techniques of drawing different materials with texture by using a pencil.

6.1

Window and opening on masonry wall (pencil)

6.2

Window on masonry wall (pencil)

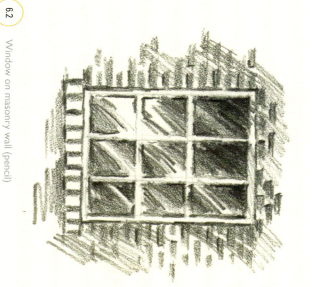

Windows are architectural components, and part of the exterior of the building as well as the interior space, and therefore add more interest and complexity to your drawing. This demonstration will show some basic techniques for drawing windows with a pencil. Usually there is considerable variation in the tonal values of the window panes. Sometimes the reflection of sunlight makes them look pure white, and other times they may appear with a gray cast. The window panes in your drawing can be varied by the way strokes are rendered and by leaving white on the paper. Window mullions usually are left with white. Figures 6.1 and 6.2 are two examples of drawing windows from an exterior view. Figure 6.1 is an example of window panes and openings. Figure 6.2 is an example of window panes with sunlight reflection.

For rendering a window from an interior view, usually the window panes are left white or very light gray. The window mullions are gray with some emphasis in black. Sometimes you have to use skip lines to draw the window mullions in order to present the sense of light coming through the window. It is just the opposite of the way the window is presented from an exterior view. Figure 6.3 is a pencil drawing that presents a window from an interior view. Figure 6.4 shows a close look at the window.

6.3

Interior space with window (pencil)

6.4   Window from interior view (pencil)

TEXTURE DEMONSTRATION #2 – DRAWING MASONRY WITH A PENCIL

Masonry is one kind of architectural material that could be used for both exteriors and interiors. Often you see a brick wall in the interior space or you see a stone wall around the fireplace. Therefore, rendering masonry with the right technique is important for sketching. The desired effect of rendering a brick or stone is to give it a true appearance without painstaking and time-consuming work and without making the drawing look mechanical. Therefore, it is not necessary to draw every single brick or stone, but rather a random sampling to make your sketch look finished. Here are some simple steps for creating bricks:

1. Use 45 pencil strokes to have a tone of the shaded area massed-in as an undertone.

2. Some areas are left untouched, while others are filled in with individual bricks against a light background.

3. Draw some individual bricks with a variety of values, usually the emphasis is put along the edges, such as the opening edge of the fireplace. The emphasis means showing more individual bricks.

4. Use a thin line to give a shadow line to a few of the bricks.

In general, the broad strokes will help to provide some character and nuance to the wall. The following are examples of rendering masonry with pencil. Figure 6.5 is a rendering with pencil of a masonry wall with door and window. Figure 6.6 is a rendering showing a masonry fireplace.

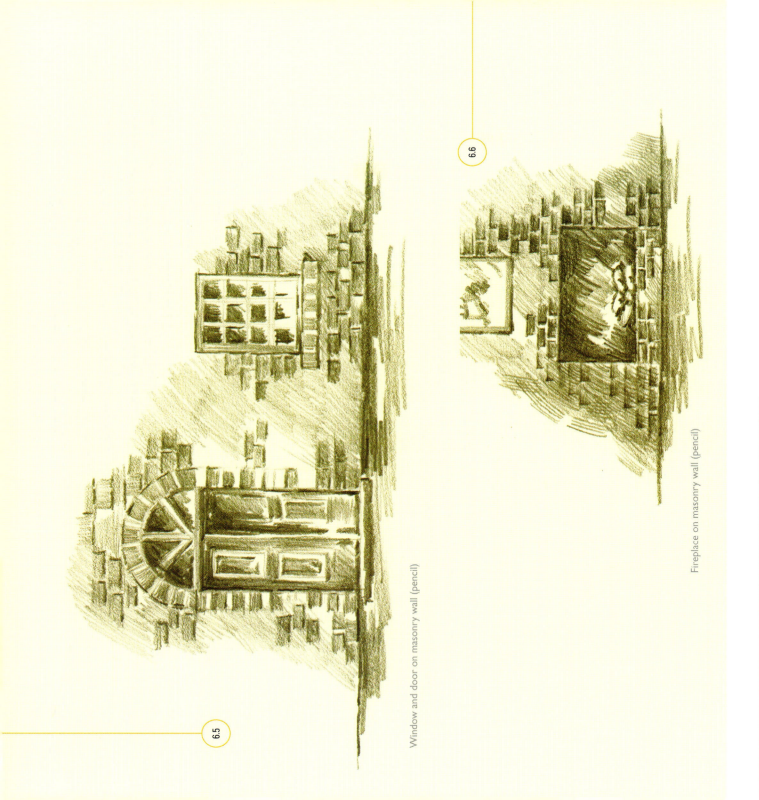

Window and door on masonry wall (pencil)

Fireplace on masonry wall (pencil)

HERE ARE SOME HINTS FOR RENDERING A MASONRY WALL

- Use broad strokes.

- Use both vertical and horizontal strokes.

- Underline some of the stones or bricks.

- In a large wall area, avoid picking out too many stones or bricks.

- Avoid too much accent on stone joints.

- Leave some white areas.

The roof is always an important component of any architectural drawing. As a designer, you should carry a sketchbook wherever you go. Sketching impressive architecture, both interior and exterior, will hone your skills as a designer. Roofs that are close to you can be rendered with considerable detail, but roofs that are farther away from you are too small in scale for any detailed treatment. They can be treated only as tonal masses. Usually the rendering of the roof is more effective when shingles or tiles do not cover the entire area. Leaving white not only avoids monotony but gives a strong suggestion of sunlight. Figure 6.7 shows an example of rendering roof tile with a pencil. In this drawing, only roof tiles that along the roof edge are drawn. An area of white is left to present sunlight reflection.

Ceiling design is an integral part of interior design. Presenting ceilings appropriately is important for interior drawing. Figure 6.8 presents an interior space of the nave of San Lorenzo in Florence, Italy, designed by Filippo Brunelleschi. The ceiling is designed as a coffer ceiling with elaborate decorations. The key point for this drawing is to have a variety of values for the ceiling in order to create a sense of distance. It is not necessary to draw each square on the ceiling. Instead, simply add more details to the portion of ceiling that is close to the viewer. Another technique used in this drawing is using crosshatch to present arch openings.

Figure 6.9 presents a sloped ceiling with skylights. Leaving a white area on the paper to create a sense of the sunbeams coming through the skylight is an important feature of this drawing. There are different values on the ceiling materials; for example, the wood rafters are much lighter than the rest of the materials. The can lights need to be different sizes to show the effect of perspective. The can light that is close to the viewer should be the biggest, while the one farther away from the viewer should be the smallest.

Figure 6.10 shows an interior space in Albrechtsburg Castle in Meissen, Germany. The tall, irregular vaults show the characteristics of Gothic architecture. In order to convey the sense of three-dimensional form for the vault ceiling, different values are presented, and the outlines of the vault are blended in with different values. Therefore, you do not see the outlines for each vault. The emphasis (or darker value) is placed on the transition edge of two surfaces.

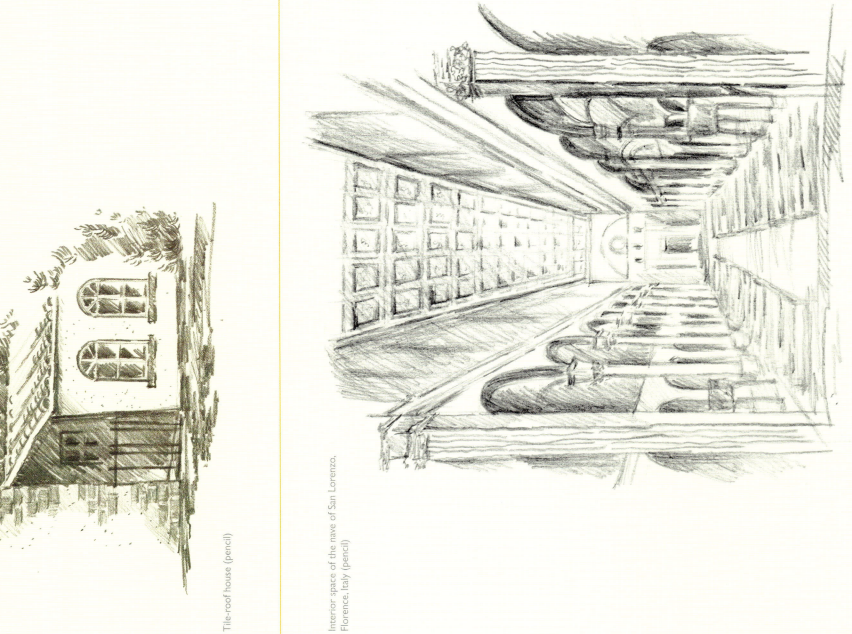

6.7 Tile-roof house (pencil)

6.8 Interior space of the nave of San Lorenzo, Florence, Italy (pencil)

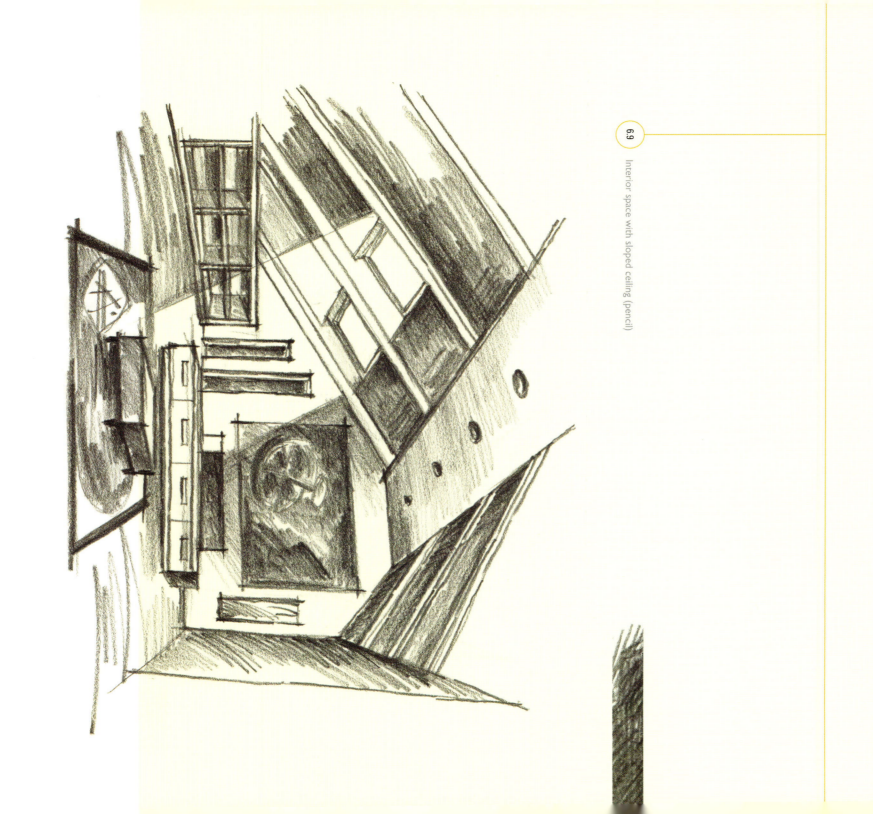

6.10

Gothic interior space with vault ceiling in Albrechtsburg Castle, Meissen, Germany (pencil)

TEXTURE DEMONSTRATION #4—DRAWING SHADOW WITH A PENCIL

Many artists have commented that the success of a sketch depends more upon the rendering of its shadows than any of its other parts. Shadows create the patterns of brightness and darkness, which is an important factor of vitality. Shadows define the form. The tonal value of cast shadows depends on the value of the surface on which the shadows fall. Showing the value changes in shadow areas is recommended. Although a plane may be in the shadow area, it usually gets reflected light from an adjacent wall.

Figures 6.11 and 6.12 show two examples of rendering shadows with pencil. You can see from other drawings that the shadow area is transparent because of the reflections. In order to present a transparent shadow, a variety of values created by a variety of strokes is used.

6.11

Entrance in shadow (pencil)

THE FOLLOWING ARE SOME HINTS FOR RENDERING SHADOWS

- Make the shadow the darkest at the edge of light.

- Usually avoid outlines on shadows.

- Usually present reflected light from the adjacent wall.

- Carefully draw shadows to define form.

- Make accent shadows where shadow meets light.

- Make the shadow transparent, with a variety of values.

6.12   Wall opening in shadow (pencil)

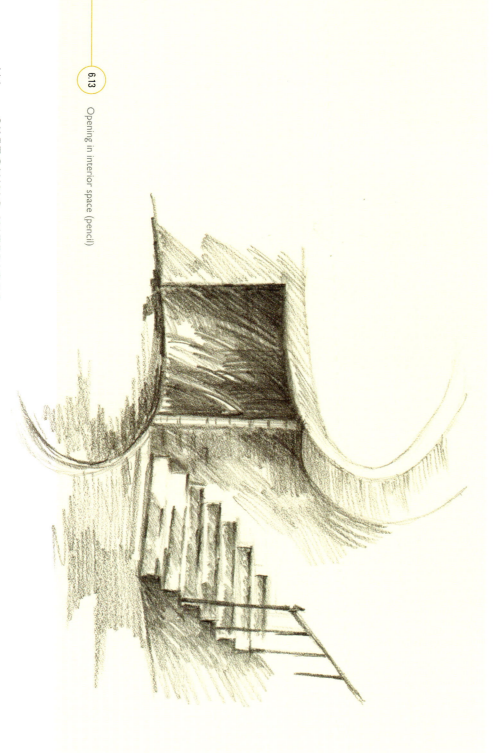

TEXTURE DEMONSTRATION #5 — DRAWING OPENINGS WITH A PENCIL

Often you will find wall openings in both interior and exterior sketches. Openings on the wall in an interior space could be a hall-way entrance or a vestibule that connects another space. Therefore, rendering the openings with appropriate technique is critical for sketching. An open door frequently appears as an unbroken dark area. If you treat it as you would sketch a flat surface without a variety of values and strokes, it will look uninteresting and not atmospheric. It is better to break up the area with pencil strokes that vary both in value and direction. You should also leave some white areas or glimpses of clear white paper between strokes.

Figures 6.13 and 6.14 show examples of rendering openings. Figure 6.13 is an interior opening by a staircase. The technique uses a variety of pencil strokes. The strokes are varied in value and direction. Leaving white area on the paper to show reflections is critical.

Figure 6.14 shows an interior view of a late Gothic church in Antwerp, the Netherlands. The opening space at the arch is drawn with a variety of pencil strokes, using different directions and values. Vertical lines are used extensively to present the primary characteristic of Gothic architecture, such as the pointing arch and vault of vertical and upward movement reaching toward the sky. Although the vertical lines are wiggly, they present the sense of human touch and imperfection that is one of the characteristics of freehand sketching.

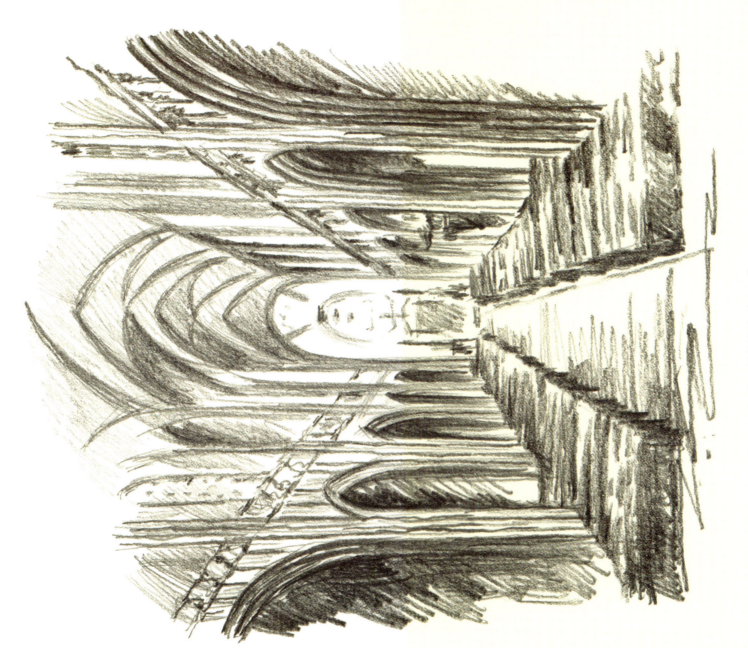

Interior view of a late Gothic church in Antwerp church in the Netherlands (pencil)

6.14

EXERCISE

6.1

EXPLORING WINDOWS AND MASONRY

This exercise allows you to explore how to render windows and masonry. Using Figure 6.15 as a model, sketch stones by presenting different tonal values, as introduced in the demonstrations about how to present bricks in this chapter. The techniques of presenting stones and bricks are very similar. Figure 6.16 shows a photo of a window by a masonry wall. Use the masonry drawing technique you learned in Texture Demonstration #2 for drawing a brick wall. Practice how to render a window from an interior view.

Interior room view (Photo © Caruntu/Shutterstock)

6.16

Window by a masonry wall (Photo © Preservation Works Ltd., www.preservationworks.us)

EXERCISE

6.2

INTERIOR PERSPECTIVE—EXPLORING SHADOWS AND OPENINGS

This exercise will help you to practice how to render shadows and openings. Figure 6.17 shows an interior perspective photo of a room in shadow. You will need to use various strokes to render the openings and shadows with different tonal values. Figure 6.18 is another interior perspective, where white predominates. Leaving white on the paper is critical for this drawing. Render the shadows in different tonal values with a variety of strokes.

Interior space, room in shadow (Photo courtesy of Holman House, Architects: Durbach Block Architects. Photograph: Chris Cole)

6.17

6.18

Interior space, with arch openings
(Photo © Bernardo Grijalva/iStockphoto)

PRESENTING TEXTURE WITH INK

Usually ink is the favored medium for artists who like to sketch when traveling. A Sharpie is best tool for this purpose. Here are some simple demonstrations to follow in order to learn some techniques for drawing different materials with texture using ink (Sharpie).

It is critical to be able to master basic strokes as a prerequisite to any other drawing skills. It is impossible to further develop drawing techniques without basic pen control. Practicing these basics might seem to be boring and unexciting, but they are fundamental and must be practiced before you can continue with some of the later drawings in this chapter. Examine the pen strokes in Figures 6.19, 6.20, and 6.21a and b. Each stroke has direction. Each stroke must be laid down with determination and preplanning. Notice the difference between the strokes made using even pressure and those made using varied pressure, as shown in Figure 6.21a.

In addition to the textures shown in Figures 6.19, 6.20, and 6.21a, Figure 6.21b presents different examples of crosshatching. The sphere is drawn by using hook lines in order to convey the sense of circular surface with different tonal values. The value bar is drawn by a combination of vertical, horizontal, and diagonal lines. The darker value can be achieved by using more varieties of combinations. The rest of the crosshatching examples are drawn by using diagonal lines with different angles as well as vertical or horizontal lines.

When you travel and carry a sketchbook with you, you always want to draw the most fascinating scene you encounter.

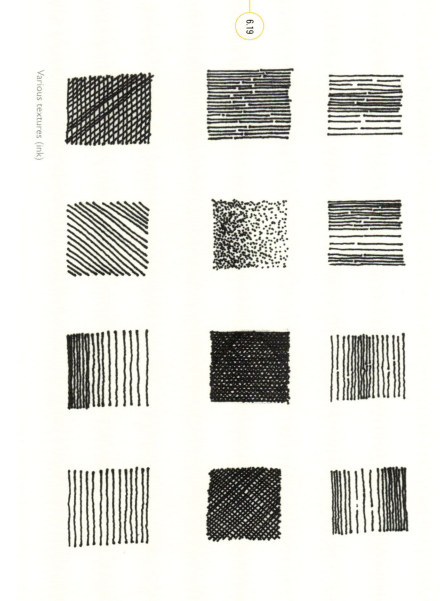

6.19

Various textures (ink)

Various values on cubes (ink)

6.20

Various textures of ink

6.21a

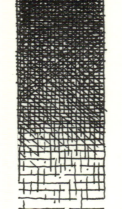
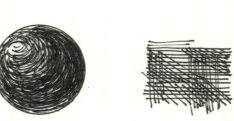

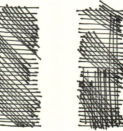

Various shadings and crosshatching in ink

6.21b

DEMONSTRATION #7—DRAWING LANDSCAPING WITH INK (SHARPIE)

Drawing landscaping is critical for exterior sketching because well-executed landscaping will make your sketches more attractive. Figure 6.22 presents two examples of how to sketch bushes. The techniques are the same as when using pencils or markers. You always want to present a variety of values on the object in order to suggest volume. Try to imagine that bushes are simple geometric forms, such as a sphere with irregular edges. The variety values can be achieved by using the ink texture shown in Figures 6.22 and 6.23. You also can refer to Chapter 9 for examples of landscapes drawn with markers.

Figure 6.23 shows a good example to follow for sketching trees. Trunks should be cylindrical with irregular edges. Drawing lines will add some texture to the trunk. Adding more lines, both skip lines and wiggly ones, on both sides will increase the value. A cluster of leaves might look like a sphere with an irregular shape. Adding some darker values with ink underneath the cluster of leaves will give the tree some texture and present a sense of three-dimensional form. The addition of some floating leaves will make your drawing even more alive. Do not forget to draw ground, even just a few simple lines with shadows. Figure 6.24 shows trees integrated into an architectural sketching of old cathedral in downtown St. Louis, Missouri.

Landscape (ink)

6.22

Trees (ink)

6.23

6.24

Architectural sketching—Old Cathedral in downtown St. Louis, Missouri (ink)

It is difficult to show shadows and openings appropriately with ink, especially for beginners. Therefore, it is important to practice mastering the techniques of drawing shadows and openings, or your drawings will look stiff and lack vitality. The techniques for using ink are similar to those for pencil. You can use crosshatching to achieve a variety of values. The crosshatching could be varied in direction and density. Density means that the ink strokes are piled up very closely or layered with bigger gaps. Figures 6.25a and 6.25b demonstrate the techniques of drawing shadows and openings.

Figure 6.25a shows another example of Gothic architecture, the Lübeck Cathedral in Germany. Vertical, wiggly lines are used extensively in order to present the characteristics of Gothic architecture. The opening area under the arch is drawn by crosshatching. You can see the variety of tonal values. In the shaded area, crosshatching is used to increase darker values.

Figure 6.25b presents another interior space of Gothic architecture in Germany. It is the Church of St. Martin in Landshut. The church was built first by Hanns Krammernauer with complex vault. The techniques used in this drawing are similar to those in Figure 6.25a.

Figure 6.26a is the monumental staircase in Upper Belvedere Palace, Vienna, and a good example of Baroque design. The characteristics of Baroque architecture are rich, with excessive decoration, displaying a sense of movement and drama, as shown through the use of spirals, twisted columns, and curved lines. In drawing, using curved lines and squiggly lines can express the Baroque characteristics effectively. Crosshatching is used extensively for openings and the background. Figure 6.26b shows interior of the dome of St. Peter's Basilica, Vatican City, Rome, which is also an example of Baroque style. Details include different types of crosshatching for openings and shadows as well as hook lines on columns and circular surfaces.

**DEMONSTRATION #8 – DRAWING SHADOWS
AND OPENINGS WITH INK (SHARPIE)**

Interior space of a Gothic architecture—the Lübeck Cathedral in Germany (ink)

Interior space of a Gothic architecture—the Church of St. Martin in Landshut, Germany (ink)

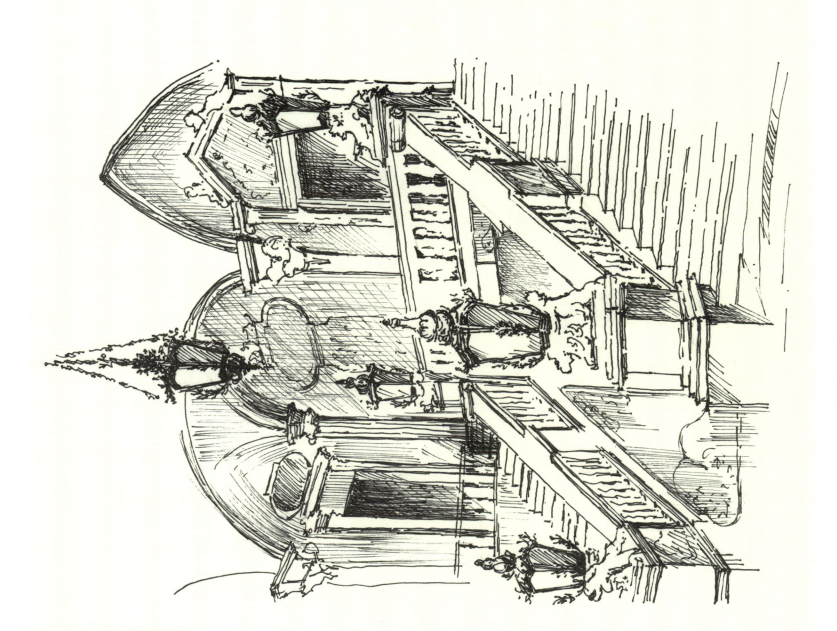

Baroque–style interior space—Upper Belvedere Palace, Vienna (ink)

6.26a

Baroque-style interior space – St. Peter's Basilica, Vatican City (ink)

6.26b

EXERCISE

6.3

EXPLORING OPENINGS—SHADOWS AND LANDSCAPING WITH BOTH PENCIL AND INK (SHARPIE)

1. Use pencil to draw the photo shown in Figure 6.27. Pay attention to different materials and shadows. Use various strokes to present different values. Figure 6.28 shows the photo sketched in pencil.

2. Use Sharpie to draw an ink drawing in Figure 6.29. Use different ink strokes to present different values for the trees. Pay attention to crosshatching on walls and openings, as well as shadows on the ground.

6.27

Street scene—Lucca, Tuscany, Italy (Photo courtesy of MA Andrew, www.picturesforwalls.com)

TIPS AND HINTS

● The same value concepts apply in ink drawing as in pencil drawing. Using a Sharpie, you need to present a variety of values on the object and in the shadow area.

● To make a darker value in ink drawings, you will need to use more condensed ink strokes in the darker area.

● Use different strokes in different densities and directions to present different tonal values in the shadow area.

Street scene sketch—Lucca, Tuscany, Italy (pencil)

6.28

6.29

Street scene sketch (ink)

SUMMARY

In this chapter, you:

- Were shown how to use a pencil to render different materials, such as bricks and stones, and architectural components, such as windows, ceilings, and roofs.

- Learned techniques of rendering shadows and openings with pencil and Sharpie.

- Practiced how to control a pen to present different values.

- Practiced how to master a pen to draw basic strokes.

- Had the chance to draw perspectives both from a photo and a site.

In general, it does not matter if you choose to use a pencil or Sharpie; the same guidelines for rendering different values are applicable. You need to use various types of strokes to render different tonal values on the surface of the object and in the shadow area, as well as to show openings in rooms and buildings.

KEY TERMS

Crosshatching	Drawing Glasses/Windows	Drawing Openings	Drawing Shadows
Drawing Bricks	Drawing Interior Ceiling	Drawing Roofs	Drawing Stone

ADDITIONAL EXERCISES

1. Chose any drawing that you prefer from this chapter. Use pencil or Sharpie to redraw it. The purpose of this exercise is to practice pencil and ink sketching techniques.

2. Go to your favorite interior space to sketch with either a pencil or Sharpie. Pay attention to your perspective and make sure it is accurate. It is important to create contrast for values on the objects that comprise your focal point. Use different strokes to present texture for materials.

7

PRESENTING MATERIALS WITH MARKERS

Color is the ultimate expression for artists. Color plays an important part in the everyday work of designers. Color principles are the same for most media, such as watercolors or colored pencils used for renderings, and only the principles of application change. Markers are used extensively in interior and architectural rendering. Combining markers and colored pencils enables you to show different materials and components in your drawing. In this chapter you will learn how to present materials such as stones, wood, windows with draperies, and furniture by using markers, Sharpies, and colored pencils.

The use of markers is different from using pencil, ink, or colored pencils. Here is where the real fun begins—rendering your drawing with markers. Be sure your markers are fresh and moist. You always want to put the caps on your markers after you use them. Now, the very first step is to get familiar with markers and their names.

INTRODUCTION OF MARKERS

The following simple demonstrations will introduce you to the different marker types and colors that will be used often, as well as how to render different materials with markers.

Figure 7.1 shows two different markers. The top one is a Prisma-color marker and the bottom one is a Chartpak marker. Both are used in the following demonstrations and the exercises in this book. With Chartpak markers it is easy to blend different colors. You can achieve an effect that is similar to watercolor drawing, especially when you render trees with Chartpak markers. Prismacolor mark-ers are somewhat drier than Chartpak markers. If you need wide or narrow marker strokes in your drawing, Prismacolor markers are good choices. In Figure 7.1, the background is created by using a Prismacolor marker. Figures 7.2 and 7.3 show marker colors that are used often.

Shown in Figure 7.2 are Chartpak: (1) Violet Light, (2) Sapphire Blue, (3) Sky Blue, (4) Blue Glow, (5) Willow Green, (6) Grass Green, (7) Nile Green, (8) Pale Indigo, (9) Maize, (10) Buff, (11) Sunset Pink, (12) Suntan, (13) Beige, (14) Cool Gray #1, (15) Brick Red, and (16) Cool Gray #5.

In Figure 7.3, they are Prismacolor markers: (1) Cool Grey 20%, (2) Warm Grey 20%, (3) Warm Grey 30%, (4) Light Peach, (5) Light Walnut, (6) Goldenrod, and (7) Sienna Brown.

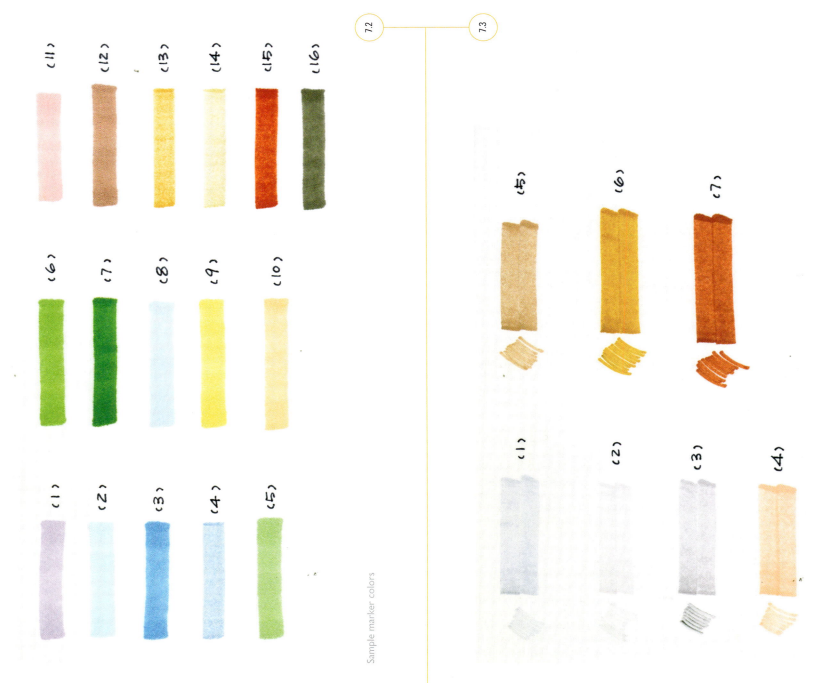

(1)
(2)
(3)
(4)
(5)

(6)
(7)
(8)
(9)
(10)

(11)
(12)
(13)
(14)
(15)
(16)

7.2

7.3

(1)
(2)
(3)
(4)

(5)
(6)
(7)

Both Chartpak and Prismacolor brand markers are used for the drawings in this book. You can add more colors to your toolbox based on your needs. Practicing different marker strokes with both wide-tip (chiseled shape) and thin-tip markers is recommended. Figure 7.4 shows some different marker strokes. Some of the strokes are created by twisting the markers, and others are straight strokes. You also can see that some of the strokes are created with thin-tip markers (Prismacolor). When you use Chartpak markers, you can twist the chiseled tip to get the thin tip. Practicing these strokes will help you work through the following demonstrations.

Presenting different values on objects in your drawing will give the sense of distance and volume. Just like pencil and ink, markers can be used to show different values. You also can use colored pencils along with markers to increase the darker values. Figure 7.5 shows cubes with different values and shadows. Pay attention to the value of the dark side of the cube and the shadow, because it is common to draw them without enough contrast.

DEMONSTRATION #2 – USING MARKERS TO PRESENT DIFFERENT VALUES

continued from previous page

● Using Figure 7.5 as a model, draw six cubes with your pencil—three rows of two cubes each. Make sure the perspectives are accurate.

● The surfaces of the cubes in the first row should be bright. The two side surfaces should have a different value. The shadows should be darker than the vertical surfaces, showing some reflections. (Note the value changes in the shadow areas in the top row of Figure 7.5.) On the second cube of the top row, use a thin Sharpie to add some vertical lines in order to increase the darker value on that surface. Just be careful that the line length is varied. You also can add some dots to increase the value.

● For cubes in the second row, draw the first one with a soft light representation, using a combination of bright surface and highlight surface. Add some vertical lines to the front of the cube in order to increase the value, using a thin Sharpie. Add some horizontal lines in the shadow area, again to highlight different values. The adjacent cube should show some darker reflections, which you can accomplish by filling in the shadow area with black.

● The cubes in the third row should show a soft lighting condition by the addition of more reflections and an increased tonal value with some vertical lines on the surface. Adding some horizontal lines in the shadow area will also create that effect. By increasing the density of lines, you can increase the value. In this case, the vertical lines can be more condensed than the horizontal lines. The second cube in the third row should show a dark vertical face by filling in the area with a gray marker and filling the shadow area with black. You also can add more vertical lines on one of the vertical surfaces. In this demonstration, using only gray and black markers is recommended.

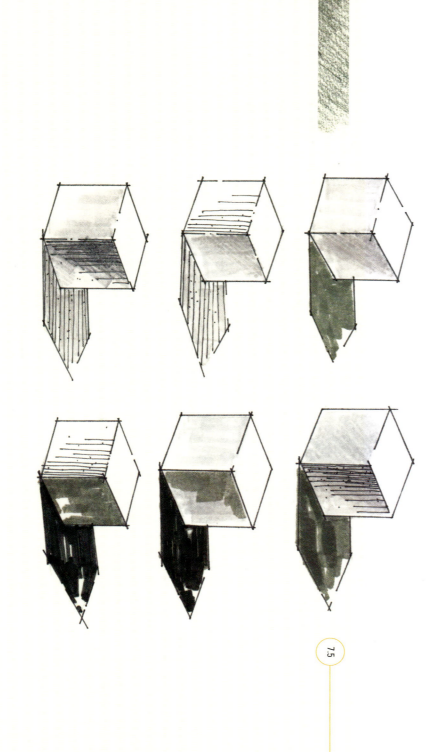

Cubes with different values (marker, ink)

7.5

In order to show a curved surface, you will have to use a variety of values. Again, the same principles used for pencil and ink drawings will apply here. Figures 7.6, 7.7, and 7.8 show examples of a simple container rendered with markers and Sharpies. In these drawings, you can see that different values are created with ink lines and shadings of gray and black markers. Then, on top of the markers, ink lines are added in order to increase the darker values. You also can see that skip lines are used in the drawings. A thicker Sharpie is used to define the edge that is closer to the viewer.

1. Use pencil to sketch the outlines of the container. Make sure that the perspective is accurate.

2. Use lighter gray markers to add values on the container.

3. Use darker gray markers to add values in the darker area as well as at the edge of the container.

4. Use a black marker to add the darkest value. Be careful not to add too much black.

5. Use a black marker to add darker value for the shadow. You may want to leave some white showing.

6. Use a thin Sharpie to trace the edge of the container. Remember to use skip lines; your eyes will fill in the blanks.

7. Use a thicker Sharpie to define the edge of the container that is closest to you, and further define the edge with skip lines.

8. Use Sienna Brown Prismacolor marker to draw some parallel strokes in order to present the floor.

DEMONSTRATION #3 — PRESENTING DIFFERENT VALUES ON A CURVED SURFACE WITH MARKERS

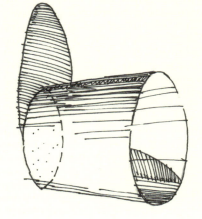

Bucket (ink)

7.6

Bucket (marker, ink)

7.7

Buckets (marker, ink)

7.8

You will see wood everywhere in an interior space, such as wood wall panels, a wood table, or wood benches. To be able to present wood material with markers is an important skill for designers. The key for presenting wood is to show wood grains appropriately on a surface. Wood grains can be drawn with colored pencils, using skip lines or dashed lines. Figure 7.9 shows a wood chair rendered with markers. Figure 7.10 shows a wood bench. It is important to use straight marker strokes to represent the wood planks. The procedure of creating the drawings in Figures 7.9 and 7.10 are as follows:

1. Use a pencil to sketch an accurate perspective.

2. Use a lighter marker to render the chair and the bench. The marker used here is a Chartpak (Buff color).

3. Use Prismacolor markers (Sienna Brown, Goldenrod) to draw marker strokes as wood planks. Make sure to leave some white showing.

4. Use a gray marker to render the background.

5. Use gray or black markers to render the shadow. It is usually best not to outline the shadow, but this suggestion depends on the style of the drawing. Sometimes you can add outlines such as in Figures 7.9 and 7.10.

6. Use a thin Sharpie to add some lines. You also can add some dots to increase the value.

7. Use a thicker Sharpie to add some thicker lines for the bench.

DEMONSTRATION #4—PRESENTING WOOD AND BENCHES WITH MARKERS

Wooden bench (marker, ink)

Wooden chair (marker, ink)

7.10

7.9

continued from previous page

Figure 7.11 shows a wall panel with wood grain. The procedure to create this drawing is as follows:

1. Use pencil to sketch the outline of the object. Make sure that the perspective is accurate.

2. Use a light-colored marker (Chartpak, Buff color) for the first layer.

3. Use a colored pencil or Prismacolor marker (Sienna Brown) to add the wood-grain texture. Use dashed lines and skip lines for this. You also can twist your colored pencil for different line widths.

4. Use a colored pencil to add darker values on the object. You can use 45-degree pencil strokes. Make sure to leave an area out in order to present the reflection on the wood. It will make your drawing look more realistic.

5. Use a Sharpie to draw an outline of the object. Add darker value in the dark side.

6. Use a Prismacolor marker to add strokes on top of the panel.

7. Use a gray marker to render the background by using larger strokes, as shown in Figure 7.11.

Figures 7.12 and 7.13 are two examples of an interior space that has wood wall panels or other wood finishes. Use these examples to create some interiors with wood finishes.

7.11

Wood panel on wall (marker, ink, colored pencil)

Interior space with wood panels (marker, ink, colored pencil)

7.12

Interior space with wood finishes (marker, ink, colored pencil)

7.13

DEMONSTRATION #5—DRAWING MASONRY WALL WITH MARKERS

Again, the same principles used in Chapter 6 (Demonstration #2) for drawing masonry with pencils will apply for markers. The desired effect when drawing brick or stone is to give it a true-to-life appearance. Therefore, it is necessary to draw bricks randomly and in different widths and lengths to simulate the rough structure usually found in this material. It is not necessary to draw every single brick or stone, and leaving some out will enhance the effect. You can also use colored pencils to add values in darker areas as needed. Figure 7.14 shows a photo of a fireplace used as a reference to create a drawing of it (Figure 7.15). Figure 7.16 shows a detail of a masonry wall, while Figure 7.17 shows the same masonry wall in the context of an interior space.

Here is a simple procedure to follow for creating a masonry wall:

1. Sketch out the perspective in pencil. An accurate perspective is important.

2. Use markers to lay out the color tone for the masonry wall. Make sure to leave some white spaces on the paper.

3. Use ink to draw some of the stones/bricks. Pay attention to the shape of stones; they should be varied in shape and size, but still maintain a realistic look.

4. Use some similar-colored pencils to add value to each of the stones. Add more emphasis underneath the stone with other colors. You also can use some markers for adding extra value to each stone.

5. Use a thicker Sharpie to add black shadow underneath single stones. Add shadows randomly to only some of the stones, not every one. Make sure to add shadows along the edge of the masonry wall.

6. Use colored pencils or lighter markers to draw some strokes along the masonry wall.

Fireplace (Photo © Tomasz Markowski/Shutterstock)

7.16 Stone wall (marker, ink, colored pencil)

7.17 Interior space with stone wall (marker, ink, colored pencil)

Rendering windows from an interior view is important for interior perspective. Mastering this skill makes your interior perspective drawings more lifelike. Figure 7.18 is an interior photo that shows off the window and drapery treatment. Figure 7.19 duplicates that photo as a drawing. The window mullions here behind the curtains are shown using skip lines with light gray markers. When you layout the first layer of marker on sofas, leaving white on paper to present the highlight. Use colored pencil and ink strokes to present a variety of values on a sofa in order to create curved surface on sofa backs and arms, as well as cushions.

Here is a simple procedure to follow for rendering drapery (see Figure 7.20):

1. Use a pencil to draw the outline of the window and the drapery.

2. Decide on a color palette for the drawing. Start with the lightest color. Make sure to leave some white space.

3. Use a darker marker to add darker values in the fold areas on the curtain.

4. Use colored pencils to add more values in shadow areas.

5. Use a Sharpie to outline the drapery for a finished look. Use some wiggly lines when drawing the folds of the drapery.

6. Use colored pencils only to draw sheered curtain.

Window with drapery (Photo © Stéphane Bidouze/iStockphoto)

Interior space with window and drapery
(marker, ink, colored pencil)

7.18

7.19

7.20

Window drapery (marker, ink, colored pencil)

continued from previous page

Here is a simple procedure for rendering a window from an interior view (see Figure 7.21):

1. Use a pencil to sketch the outline of the window. Make sure that the perspective is accurate.

2. Use lighter markers (Chartpak, Willow Green, and Sapphire Blue colors) to render the exterior scene. It should be subtle.

3. Use a light gray marker to draw the window mullions. Use skip lines for this.

4. Use a marker to render the surrounding materials, such as the bricks on top of the window.

5. Use a thin Sharpie to add definitions on some of the window mullions and bricks. (Not every single one of them.)

6. Add shadows with a thin Sharpie and background with markers.

7.21

Window from an interior view (marker, ink, colored pencil)

Furniture is always an integral part of interior space. To be able to present furniture with markers effectively is critical for designers. Figures 7.22 and 7.24 are photographic examples of sofas you might find in an interior space. Figures 7.23 and 7.25 reproduce them as drawings.

The process for rendering a sofa or chair can be summarized as follows:

1. Draw an outline of the furniture with pencil or colored pencil. Make sure your perspective is accurate.

2. Decide on the colors for the furniture, and start with the lighter colors.

3. Leave some white on the paper when using markers.

4. Use colored pencils to add darker values if needed.

5. Use colored pencils or ink to create shadows. Make sure to show a variety of values in the shadow areas.

6. Use a Sharpie to outline the furniture and add finishing touches to your drawing.

DEMONSTRATION #7—RENDERING FURNITURE WITH MARKERS

SKETCHING INTERIORS

Sofa (marker, ink, colored pencil)

7.23

Sofa (Photo © Alexey Kashin/iStockphoto)

7.22

7.24

Sofa (Photo © Lifestyle Solutions)

7.25

Sofa (marker, ink, colored pencil)

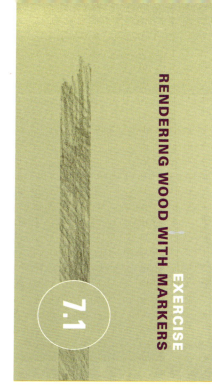

RENDERING WOOD WITH MARKERS

EXERCISE

7.1

This exercise will help you to practice rendering wood with markers. Use Figure 7.26 as inspiration for a drawing of a wood wall panel. You will need to use markers to render the drawing with different tonal values. Showing wood grains correctly is important for this drawing.

7.26 Wooden wall panel (Photo courtesy of Grant Govier/Red Cover)

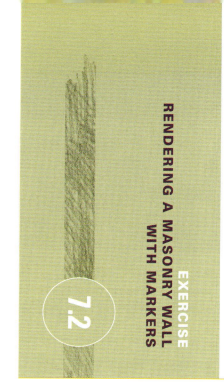

EXERCISE

RENDERING A MASONRY WALL WITH MARKERS

7.2

This exercise will let you practice rendering a masonry wall. Use Figure 7.27 as a reference for a sketch. Sketch bricks/stones by presenting different tonal values as introduced in Demonstration #2 in this chapter. Make sure your perspective is accurate.

7.27

Interior space with masonry wall (Photo courtesy of Cg Advertising, http://www.cgadvertising.com)

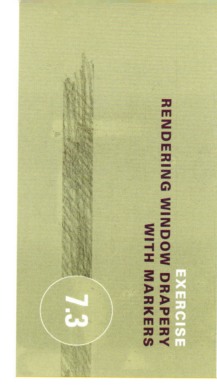

This exercise will help you to practice rendering a window with drapery from an interior view. Figure 7.28 shows an interior perspective photo to use as a reference. Use markers to render the drapery with different tonal values. Leaving white space on the paper is critical for this drawing. You also need to present darker values in order to show the folds of the drapery. Rendering a sofa is another goal of this exercise.

Interior space with drapery (Photo © Mmaeyer/Dreamstime.com)

7.28

EXERCISE

7.4

RENDERING A SOFA WITH MARKERS

This exercise will help you to practice how to render furniture. Figure 7.29 is a perspective of sofa in an interior space to use as a reference. You will need to use markers and colored pencils to render the sofa with different tonal values. Leaving white space on the paper is again critical for a realistic drawing. Pay special attention to rendering an exterior window view. It needs to be subtle in order to have a sense of distance.

Interior space with sofa (Photo © Shutterstock)

7.29

SUMMARY

In this chapter, you:

- Were introduced to how to use markers to render different materials, such as stones and wood, windows with drapery, and furniture.

- Practiced how to control a marker to present different values.

- Practiced how to render furniture with markers from photos.

- Had the chance to draw perspectives both from a photo and a site.

In general, it does not matter what kind of media you use; the same guidelines for adding tonal values to a drawing apply. You need to use various strokes to render different tonal values on the surface of the object and in the shadow area. Colored pencils can be used to add darker values.

KEY TERMS

Colored Pencils	Drawing Furniture	Focal Point	
Drawing Bricks	Drawing Stone	Markers	Twisting Your Marker
Drawing Draperies	Drawing Wood	Sharpies	

ADDITIONAL EXERCISES

1. Go to your favorite interior space where there is a mix of objects, textures, materials, and details, such as wood furniture, windows, and drapes. Sketch the area using a combination of markers, colored pencils, and Sharpies. Be conscious of all the techniques used in this chapter, like perspective, value, shading, shadows, and detail.

2. Figure 7.30 is the Zimmerman House in Manchester, New Hampshire, designed by Frank Lloyd Wright. The interior and exterior spaces flow together. The same autumnal colors are used throughout. The red brick is the signature of the design. Use markers, colored pencils, and Sharpies to render this interior space. Use the techniques of rendering a masonry wall for this drawing.

3. Figure 7.31 is a photo of a residential space. Wood planks are used on both walls and ceilings. Use the techniques of rendering wood planks with markers, colored pencils, and Sharpies to render this interior space.

7.30

Interior space with brick walls (Photo courtesy of Cindy Mackey)

Interior space with wood plank walls (Photo © Bertrand Benoit/Shutterstock)

8

INTERIOR RENDERING WITH MARKERS

A very critical step in freehand sketching is to have an accurate perspective. You should practice this technique frequently in order to master the skill of perspective drawing. In addition, knowing the important techniques for interior rendering, such as creating a quick sketch with markers, as well as different drawing styles and color combinations are important skills for designers. In this chapter, quick sketches with markers will be introduced. With more practice, you will develop your own sketching style that incorporates different color combinations and line qualities.

QUICK SKETCH WITH MARKERS

The quick sketch is very useful during the schematic design phase. It allows you to present your design concept quickly and effectively. The key point is to sketch your object and the space with accurate perspective. If the perspective and proportion are not correct at the beginning, then it is not worth spending time and effort to render the drawing.

For the quick sketch, it is not necessary to present everything in detail. You can use single-line blocks and shadows to define spatial relationship. Shadows created by light and different colors as well as textures will create the sense both of distance and three-dimensional form. Figures 8.1 and 8.2 are examples of using single line and shadow to define the object and its spatial relationships. Figures 8.3 and 8.4 are examples of quick sketches created by markers. The techniques used in Figures 8.3 and 8.4 are marker strokes and contrast at the shadow area.

Figures 8.5 and 8.6 are two quick sketches of interior spaces. They are created by the combination of marker and colored pencil as well as Sharpie. Leaving the marker strokes and pencil strokes visible in the drawing will make it look fresher and more realistic. Effectively using pencil strokes can achieve the results of a variety of values, which is very important in drawing.

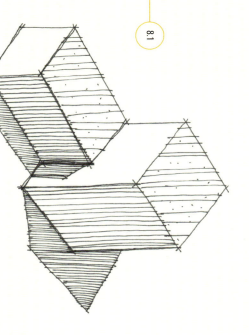

8.1   Lines and shadow to define spatial relationships (ink)

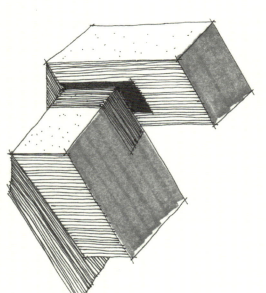

8.2   Lines and shadow to define spatial relationships (marker, ink)

Lines and shadow define spatial relationships (marker, ink)

FASHION SHOP

Lines and shadow define spatial relationships (marker, ink, colored pencil)

CONTRAST IN DRAWING

The concept of contrast was mentioned earlier in the book. Presenting contrast in your drawing is essential. The contrast can be created by different values and different colors, and will create the sense of depth. If the object is closer to you, you should have strong contrast on it. If the object is farther away from you, you should have soft contrast on it. This principle can be applied to your sketching. Figures 8.7 and 8.8 show examples of interiors where bold black markers were used at the entranceways to introduce contrast.

8.5

Interior space (marker, ink, colored pencil)

8.6 Interior space (marker, ink, colored pencil)

8.7 Using bold black markers to create contrast (marker, ink, colored pencil)

TEXTURE IN DRAWING

As introduced in Chapter 6, texture is very important to show the realism of an object or environment. Presenting texture needs careful observation and the application of the appropriate techniques using different line qualities. If it is hard to re-create a texture with markers or pens, you can use a computer program, such as Photoshop, to assist with the outcome you desire. Using Photoshop to edit a freehand drawing will be discussed in Chapter 10. Figures 8.9, 8.10, and 8.11 are examples of digital drawings that were edited using Photoshop. In Figures 8.9 and 8.10, real materials such as brick and marble are shown on elevations. In figure 8.11, wood material is shown on wood panel and furniture.

VOLUME IN DRAWING

The size and position of the object is relative in drawing. But the proportion of the object is important. Presenting different values will increase the sense of volume. Line qualities such as thick lines and thin lines can affect the object's texture and value. For example, thin lines should be used at bright areas, and thick lines should be used in dark areas. The outline of the object should be thicker, while the projection line, or inner line, should be thinner. In this way, the sense of distance and of volume can be shown. In addition, different weights of lines can be created by twisting your pen. It can make your drawing more alive.

Digital drawing edited using Photoshop

8.9

Digital drawing edited using Photoshop

8.10

Interior space (digital drawing using Photoshop)

COLOR AND LIGHT

Color and light are two important factors for color rendering of both interiors and exteriors. Understanding the fundamentals of color and light will help you to master the techniques of color rendering. Color and light always exist together in a real environment. Therefore, you should not just look at the color without considering light when you are working on a color rendering. For example, a light-blue chair might look a little bit purple on its bright surface because of warm-tone lighting, while the chair's darker surface might look like dark navy or even black, or perhaps be mixed with purple

because of the reflections from its adjacent environment. Therefore, analyzing color and light when you observe an object in interior space is a critical step.

Hue, Value, and Chroma

In the Munsell color system, any color is described by three attributes: hue, value, and chroma. That means any color can be specified by these three dimensions.

Hue The first attribute of a color is its position in the spectrum on the color wheel (Figure 8.12), called *hue*. The three primary colors—red, blue, and yellow—are the basic hues from which all other colors can be mixed.

- When two primary colors are mixed together, the secondary colors are created. The secondary hues are orange, green, and purple.

- When adjacent primary color and secondary colors are mixed together, the tertiary colors are created, such as green-yellow and blue-green.

- Hues that are opposite each other on the color wheel are called complementary colors, such as yellow and purple, orange and blue. When two complementary colors are mixed, gray is created.

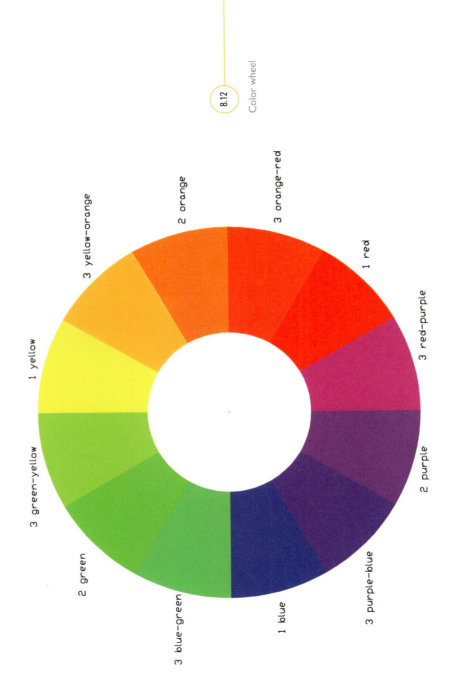

8.12 Color wheel

Value The second attribute of any color is its brightness and darkness, called value (Figure 8.13). Values create the sense of distance and depth as well as volume in a drawing. A good drawing should have different values, using light, medium, and dark shading to create spatial depth and contrast in order to present a sense of distance and three-dimensional form.

Chroma The third attribute of any color is its intensity or purity, called chroma or saturation. The most pure and intense colors are those that are not mixed with their opposite hue on the color wheel. Conversely, adding the opposite hue on the color wheel lowers the chroma of a color and makes it less pure and intense. Figure 8.13 includes a gray scale of values, from very light gray to black, and a

8.13   Value bars

value scale of reds. The clear primary red is near the center. Adding white to primary red can produce the lighter tints, while adding gray or a complementary color can produce darker shades of red.

Color and Tone

As discussed in the previous chapters in relation to pencil drawings, presenting different values is a crucial technique in drawing. A variation of tone will give a sense of three-dimensional form and a sense of distance. Value means brightness and darkness. In color rendering, successfully presenting different values still plays an important role in giving a sense of depth and volume. Adding gray or a complementary color can produce darker shades of color.

COLOR SCHEMES, COLOR COMBINATIONS, AND DRAWING STYLES

There are four different color schemes based on the Munsell color system. They are monochromatic color scheme, analogous color scheme, complementary color scheme, and triad color scheme. By using different color combinations, different drawing styles can be presented. There are three different color combinations and five different drawing styles. There might be more combinations and styles in drawings. Here some basic color combinations and drawing styles are introduced.

Four Different Color Schemes

Monochromatic Color Scheme (Figure 8.14): This is a frequently used color scheme. In a monochromatic drawing, all colors are in a wide range of chroma and value within a single hue. It makes the environment look wider and more open.

Analogous Color Scheme (Figure 8.15): This scheme achieves harmony by using hues that are close together on the color wheel. The typical analogous color scheme uses one primary color or one secondary color plus the hues adjacent to it on either side.

Complementary Color Scheme (Figure 8.16): This color scheme is achieved by using contrasting hues from the opposite sides of the color wheel. Complementary color schemes usually seem bright and dynamic. The rendering that uses a complementary color scheme usually does so to emphasize the colors and materials of a space.

Triad Color Scheme (Figure 8.17): If three different hues approximately equidistant from one another on the color wheel are chosen—red, yellow, and blue, or slightly shifted hues—they are called a triad color scheme. Triad color schemes generally reduce the intensities of all hues or most hues. A triad color scheme is often used in small areas with a mostly neutral overall scheme.

8.15

Color wheel and analogous color scheme

8.17

Color wheel and triad color scheme

Color wheel and monochromatic color scheme

8.14

Color wheel and complementary color scheme

8.16

Three Different Color Combinations

Based on the color theory introduced earlier defining monochromatic, analogous, complementary, and triad color schemes, you can use the following three different color combinations to create different drawing styles.

Limited Color Combination (Figure 8.18): In this combination, only two or three colors are chosen as main colors. It is used often in a quick sketch. Figure 8.5 is an example of using limited colors for quick interior sketching. The colors used in the figure are blue, light gray, and suntan. The rest of the colors are used as accents.

Limited color combination

Emphasis color combination

Emphasis Color Combination (Figure 8.19): In this combination a bright color is used as a main color for the main object, and the rest of the colors are gray toned. This color combination can be used for presenting the portion of a space with a special design, such as an entrance or reception area. Figure 8.20 is an example of using emphasis color for a quick interior sketch. The majority of the colors in the drawing are gray. The emphasis color is brick red (a Sienna Brown Prisma-color marker was used).

Multiple Color Combination (Figure 8.21). In a drawing using multiple color combination, different colors are spaced everywhere. It is a unique and rich color combination. It presents strong artistic atmosphere. Figure 8.6 is an example of using a multiple color combination. The colors used in the drawing are brick red, blue, and varied shades of gray and suntan.

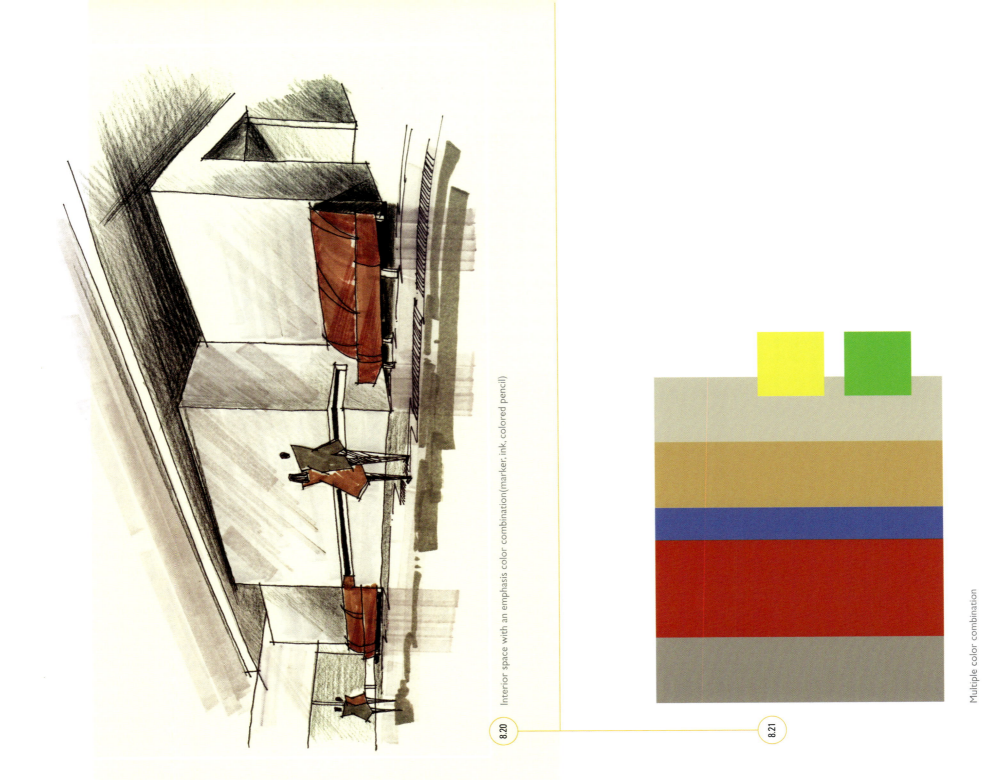

Interior space with an emphasis color combination(marker, ink, colored pencil)

8.20

Multiple color combination

8.21

Four Different Drawing Styles

Basic Style: This style uses primary, secondary, and tertiary colors combined with neutral colors. Neutral usually means without color, and neutral colors include beige, ivory, taupe, black, gray, and white. These colors appear to be without colors. In many applications, however, these hues have undercations, however, these hues have undertones of color. The drawing looks wide and stable. Most of the drawings in this book are basic styles.

Modern Style: This style uses black, white, and gray as main colors, combining with complementary colors, such as yellow and purple. The drawing looks simple and sharp (Figure 8.22).

Classical Style: This style uses a relatively darker color combination to present an elegant and quiet atmosphere. In Figure 8.23, the furniture looks relatively darker than the rest of the drawings.

Natural Style: This style uses neutral colors, as described previously, as main colors combined with lighter colors. The drawing presents a natural feeling (Figure 8.24).

8.22   Modern-style interior-space sketch using a multiple color combination (marker, ink, colored pencil)

8.23 Classical-style interior-space sketch (marker, ink, colored pencil)

8.24 Natural-style interior-space sketch (marker, ink, colored pencil)

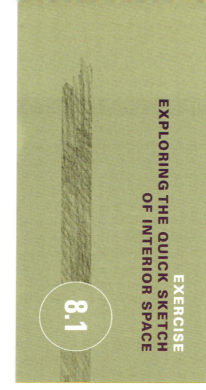

EXERCISE

EXPLORING THE QUICK SKETCH
OF INTERIOR SPACE

8.1

Sketch the interior space as shown in Figure 8.25 using markers, Sharpie, and colored pencils. Make sure that the perspective is accurate before you apply markers and colored pencils. Pay attention to color tones and the variety of values in order to present the depth of the space.

Interior space (Photo © I5 Architecture for Living, photography by Michael Jensen)

8.25

EXERCISE 8.2

EXPLORING DIFFERENT COLOR COMBINATIONS AND DRAWING STYLES

Use markers, colored pencils, and ink to sketch the space as shown in the photo in Figure 8.26. Try different color combinations and different drawing styles.

Interior space (Photo © Steven Miric/iStockphoto)

8.26

SUMMARY

In this chapter, you:

- Were exposed to making a quick sketch with markers.

- Were introduced to different color schemes and color combinations.

- Learned different drawing styles.

- Practiced creating a quick sketch with markers.

The quick sketch is very important and useful in schematic design. It conveys a designer's intent quickly and effectively. Being able to grab the main design object and sketch it in accurate perspective is the key for a good drawing. The surroundings should be simple.

KEY TERMS

Analogous Colors	Contrast	Secondary Color	Volume
Balance	Monochromatic Colors	Shadow	
Color Wheel	Munsell Color System	Texture	
Complementary Colors	Primary Color	Triad Colors	

The purpose of this chapter. Use marker, Sharpie, and colored pencils to copy that drawing on your marker paper. The purpose of this exercise is to get familiar with creating a quick sketch and using different color combinations.

2. Sketch the interior space as shown in the black-and-white photo in Figure 8.27 with different color combinations, such as limited color combination, emphasis color combination, and multiple color combination.

3. Sketch the interior space as shown in the black-and-white photo in Figure 8.28 using different color schemes, such as monochromatic colors, analogous colors, and complementary colors.

ADDITIONAL EXERCISES

1. Chose any drawing from this chapter. Use marker, Sharpie, and colored pencils to copy that drawing on your marker paper. The purpose of this exercise is to get familiar with creating a quick sketch and using different color combinations.

8.27

Interior space (Photo © Koksharov Dmitry/Shutterstock)

Interior space (Photo © Glenn Moody/Schonbek Worldwide lighting)

8.28

9

FREEHAND SKETCHING FOR PRESENTATIONS

Graphic presentation is the language designers use to communicate design concepts and ideas to clients. It is important for designers to be able to master graphic communication skills for their presentations. This chapter will walk you through the techniques to use to prepare quality presentations for a client quickly and professionally. These techniques include how to render floor plans, elevations, isometric drawings, and perspectives. The media will be markers and ink, sometimes combined with colored pencils as well. Before all these techniques are described in detail, *entourage* will be introduced because it is such an important component of rendering skills.

ENTOURAGE

A rendering such as an interior perspective or a floor plan is a major element in a presentation drawing, but it cannot stand alone. Any architectural space has surroundings, or an *entourage*. For an interior perspective, there are always people inside that space, or perhaps foliage and trees or interior landscaping. For a floor plan, depending on its location, you will find trees, bushes, grass, or even vehicles adjoining the buildings. This entourage, or surroundings, with proper

scale can enhance the quality and add more interest to your two-dimensional and three-dimensional drawings by providing your rendering with depth and scale. Because of their importance, three different entourages will be introduced in the following examples. They are trees, human figures, and cars.

Tree Presentations

In freehand sketching presentations, trees and landscaping are used as background. Therefore, it is very important to be able to present different shapes and forms of trees in order to present a vital drawing.

It is critical to understand the growing patterns of trees in general and of different varieties of them. You will need to choose an appropriate method to draw a tree. Using simple geometric form to summarize trees' basic shape and form is good basic technique. If you are able to master trees' geometric form, then you will be able to master the basic characteristics of different tree varieties. Generally speaking, for the purpose of adding entourage to design drawings, most varieties can fit into the geometric forms shown in Figures 9.1 and 9.2. Figure 9.1 presents pine trees and bushes. Figure 9.2 presents a tree with leaves and a tree with branches.

Pine Trees: Cone shape (Figure 9.1)

Bushes: A series of spheres (Figure 9.1)

Tree with leaves: Stretched sphere with irregular edge (Figure 9.2)

Tree trunks and branches: Cylinder with irregular edges (Figure 9.2)

9.1

Figure 9.1 Pine tree and bushes rendering (marker, ink)

9.2

Tree rendering (marker, ink)

In perspective and elevation drawings, tree rendering are used extensively. A perspective drawing is three-dimensional, whereas an elevation is two-dimensional. A well-drawn tree will add vitality to a sketch. Figure 9.3 presents a different elevation of a tree created by another set of techniques.

Simple Tree Elevation with Markers Figure 9.3 is a tree elevation drawn with markers and ink. It is very simple. It can be used in both perspective and elevation. Here is a quick procedure to follow:

1. Use a light green marker to draw some strokes in different directions, as shown in Figure 9.3.

2. Use a darker green marker to draw some strokes on top of the lighter green. You also can add some dots around the strokes to show floating leaves.

3. Use an Ultra Fine Point Sharpie to draw outlines of the foliage. You also can draw some small circles on top of the green dots.

TREE ELEVATION

continued from previous page

Tree Elevation with Mixed Media Figure 9.2 presents two tree renderings with mixed media. These two renderings were drawn by markers, colored pencils, and Sharpie. Here is a quick procedure to follow:

1. Use a pencil to draw a tree with a trunk and several branches.

2. Use markers to create different values on the trunk. You also can add some dots around it to show floating leaves.

3. Use colored pencil to add strokes to show shadows and textures on the trunk and branches.

4. Use a Sharpie to draw outlines of the tree and leaves. Keep in mind that it should be darker underneath the leaves because of shadow. When you need to add more value in the shadow area, you can use an Ultra Fine Point Sharpie to draw leaf texture, as introduced in Chapter 6 (Figure 6.23).

Tree Elevatios with Sharpie Figures 9.4, 9.5, and 9.6 show different shapes and forms of trees in elevation. They were drawn in ink (Ultra Fine Point Sharpie). These forms can be used in perspectives as well as elevations. Because different varieties of trees are shown, the shapes of their leaves are different. In order to increase the reality of the drawing, you can add a few leaves that are floating.

Figures 9.7 and 9.8 depict bushes. They can be used in both perspectives and elevations. They were drawn with a Sharpie. Pay attention to the different line weights by twisting your pen.

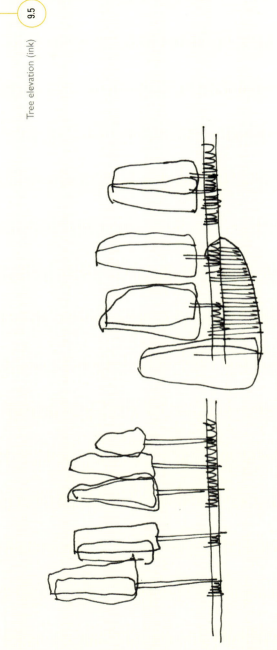

Tree elevation (ink)

9.4

Tree elevation (ink)

9.5

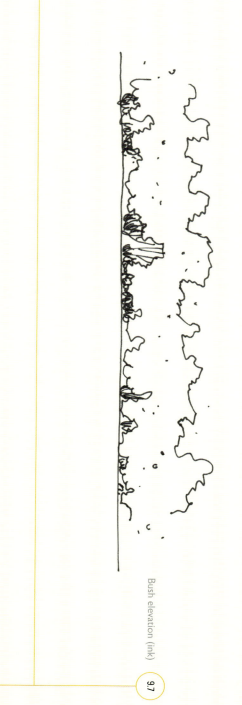

Bush elevation (ink)

9.8

Bush elevation (ink)

9.7

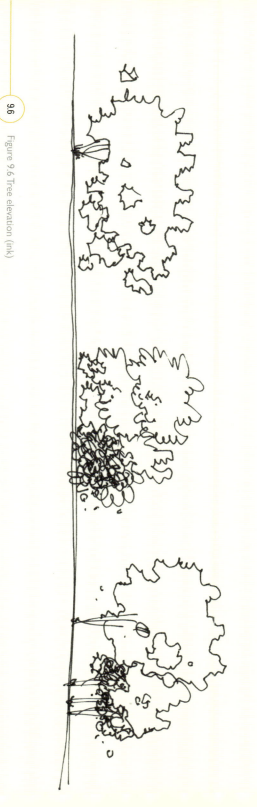

9.6

Figure 9.6 Tree elevation (ink)

continued from previous page

Tree Elevation with Markers Figures 9.9 and 9.10 present tree and bush elevations drawn by markers and Sharpie. The key point for creating these elevations is to present different values in order to present tree leaves and bushes in three-dimensional forms.

1. Use pencil to sketch the outlines of tree or bush elevations.

2. Use a light green marker to draw the top of the tree or the top of the bushes because the sunlight comes from above. When you use a marker to draw the top of the tree leaves or the bushes, you can twist your marker and leave some white on the paper. Or you can just use vertical short strokes to draw the bushes, as shown in Figure 9.10.

3. Use a darker green marker to draw the lower portion of the tree or bushes. These portions should have darker values. You also can twist your marker or use short vertical strokes. Adding floating leaves is always a good technique to make a drawing more alive.

4. Use a Sharpie to draw an outline of the tree or bushes. Do not use continuous lines to draw the entire outline; use skip lines to draw it. Your eyes will fill in the blanks.

5. Use a Sharpie to draw textures in the lower portion of the tree leaves or the bushes. Present some darker value on top of the bushes or on top of the tree leaves by adding textures, as shown in Figures 6.23 and 6.24.

6. Add shadows on the ground by using a thicker-tip Sharpie (Fine Point Sharpie). Make sure you use skip lines. You also can use a combination of colored pencils and an Ultra Fine Point Sharpie.

Bush elevation (marker, ink)

9.10

Bush elevation (marker, ink)

9.9

PLAN VIEW OF TREES

When you create a floor plan with ink or markers, adding a plan view of a tree will bring life and fun to your drawing. The basic form of a tree in plan is a circle, although there are many variations on this pattern. Figure 9.11 shows some plan views of different trees.

Tree Plan View with Sharpie

1. Use a pencil to draw a circle with a circler template. Make sure you have an appropriate scale for the circle based on the scale of your floor plan.

2. Use pencil to draw a tree plan view for the one selected from Figure 9.11.

3. Use your Sharpie to trace over your pencil lines.

4. Use a Sharpie to add shadows on the tree plan view. It provides the sense of a three-dimensional form (Figure 9.12).

Tree Plan View with Markers

1. Use a pencil to draw a circle with a circler template. Make sure you have an appropriate scale for the circle based on the scale of your floor plan.

2. Use green and yellow markers to draw on the plan view. You should leave some white on the paper.

3. Use your Sharpie to trace over your pencil lines. You also can draw some foliage on the plan view, as shown in Figure 9.12.

4. Use a thicker-tip Sharpie to add shadows on the tree plan view. It makes the trees look three dimensional (Figure 9.12).

5. Use an Ultra Fine Point Sharpie to add dots on the plan view.

Tree plan view (marker, ink)

Tree plan view (ink)

9.12

9.11

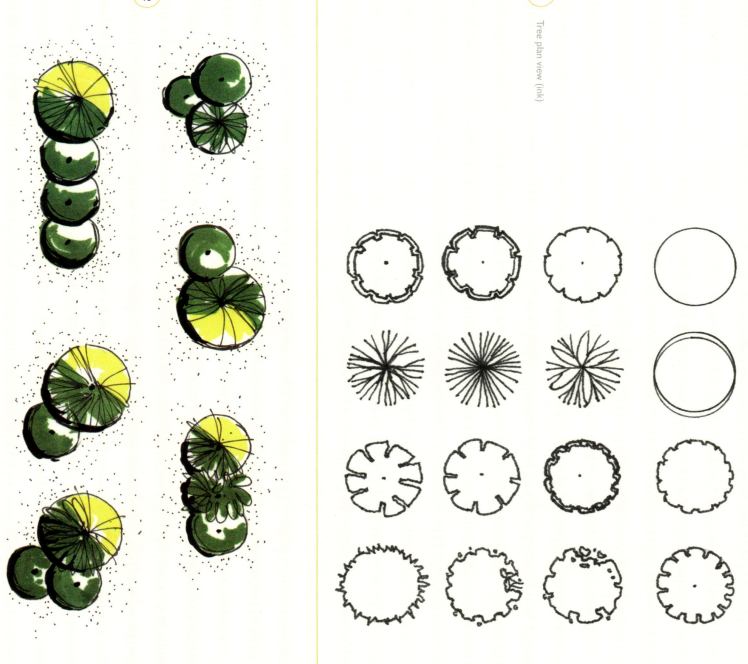

continued from previous page

Figure 9.13 is a floor plan depicting many trees in the space. By adding them to the floor plan, it presents the landscaping design and atmosphere of that interior space.

Floor plan (marker, ink)

9.13

Human figures (marker, ink)

9.14

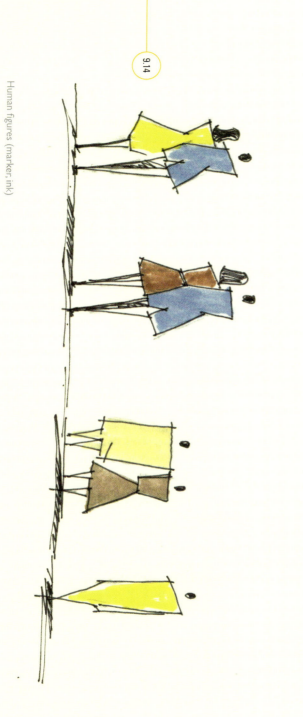

Human Figures

As indicated earlier in this chapter, it is true that interior sketches are not primarily concerned with the representation of the human figure. However, human figures do make your drawing more realistic and playful to a drawing, and they provide an immediate sense of scale to any drawing. For architectural and interior sketching, human figures should be simple and abstract because their purpose is to give a sense of scale and proportion.

The location of human figures typically will be at the entrance or at the place to which you want to draw viewers' attention. You also might want to add human figures in order to balance your drawing. The colors for human figures could be very bright or remain white depending on where you place them.

Figure 9.14 shows a few examples of sketches of human figures.

Car Presentation Drawings

In architectural renderings, a car plan view, car elevation, or car perspective is used very often. For interior sketches, there might be a chance that you need to present a car plan view or car elevation, such as a house floor plan with attached garage. Adding surroundings, such as a car, a few trees, or a pebble pavement will make your drawing more fun and vital.

Figure 9.15 shows several different ways to sketch a plan view of a car and car elevation.

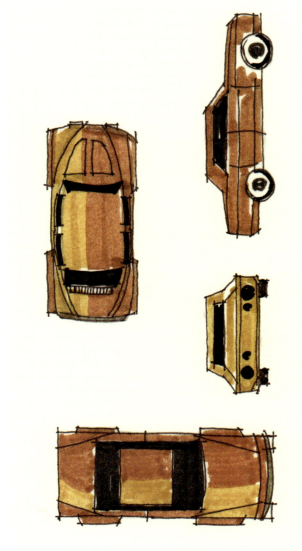

9.15 Cars: plan view, elevation (marker, ink)

FLOOR PLAN PRESENTATION

A floor plan presentation is used extensively in schematic design. Using markers and inks can help you create professional-looking floor plans quickly. It is critical to have contrasts in the drawings. Contrast could be created by using different colors and different values. Another important technique for rendering floor plans is to create a wash-like effect that makes the plan look three-dimensional. You can create gradually changing values by using a series of color markers or pencil strokes of varying weights.

The following figures are examples of floor plan presentations with markers and

Sharpies. Figures 9.16 and 9.17 are floor plans with furniture and with landscaping that surrounds the building at the entrance. Figure 9.18 is a floor plan presentation with furniture layout, landscaping, and a patio with a car outside the building. Adding the entourage makes your drawing look more realistic.

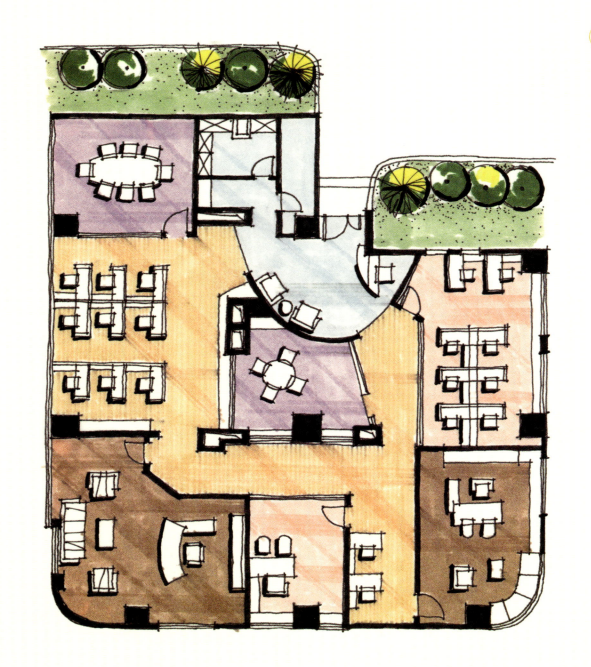

9.16

Floor plan (marker, ink)

Floor plan (marker, ink)

9.17

Floor plan (marker, ink)

9.18

continued from previous page

The major steps of rendering a floor plan as follows:

1. Use pencil to sketch the floor plan outlines, including all the furniture as well as landscaping or a car around the edges of the floor plan.

2. Use light markers to render each room. You may choose different colors to distinguish the different functions of each room.

3. Use a fine-tip marker (Prismacolor brand) to draw some horizontal or 45-degree strokes in order to add some textures and more values. Or you can use colored pencils.

4. Use a darker marker or a Sharpie to create shadows underneath the furniture in order to make the drawing look three-dimensional.

5. Use an Ultra Fine Point Sharpie to trace the pencil lines. Make sure that cross lines are used at each corner.

6. Use the Ultra Fine Point Sharpie to draw texture on tables, as shown in Figure 9.17.

7. Use the Sharpie to add definition for solid walls. It provides strong contrast and clear definition for the drawing.

8. Use marker to render the tree plan view as described previously. You do not need to color the entire tree. Leave some white paper showing. Use black, thick Sharpies to draw shadows. By adding trees in the floor plan, more interest is added to the drawing.

9. Use the Ultra Fine Point Sharpie and green markers to add dots in the grass area.

10. Use markers to render the car and add some shadows to it.

ELEVATION PRESENTATION

Elevation presentation is another method used by designers to convey their design ideas. It is two-dimensional and very easy to create. Both interior and exterior elevations have to be presented with surroundings in order to present the unity of the architecture and environment. In a schematic

design, using markers and Sharpies is an effective way to create elevation presentations quickly. The major steps of rendering an elevation are as follows:

1. Use pencil to sketch the elevations (either interior or exterior) including all the details, such as casework, furniture, and even accessories. You also can add some human figures in order to present a sense of scale and proportion.

2. Use lighter markers to render different areas of the elevation that represent different materials.

3. Combine markers with colored pencils to create texture for different materials, such as stone or wood. You do not need to draw every single piece of stone or brick. Normally, you just need to show some stones or bricks along the edges and randomly show some of them on the surface.

4. Use a fine-tip marker (Prismacolor brand) to draw some 45-degree strokes in order to add some textures and add more values. You also can use colored pencils to achieve these effects.

5. Use a darker marker or a Sharpie to create shadows at recessed areas, such as a casework or window, in order to make the drawing three- dimensional.

6. Use the Ultra Fine Point Sharpie to trace the pencil lines. Pay attention to line qualities, such as skip lines or dashed lines.

7. Use markers to render tree elevation. You do not need to color the entire tree. Leave some whites showing. Use black, thick Sharpies to draw shadows. By adding trees in elevations, you add more interest or balance to the drawing.

8. Use markers to add color to human figures. Usually the human figures are added at the place that will draw viewers' attention, such as the focal point or entrance. The colors selected usually are very bright.

Figures 9.19 and 9.20 are examples of exterior elevation presentations with markers and inks.
Figures 9.21 and 9.22 are examples of interior elevations.

9.19

Exterior elevation plan (marker, ink)

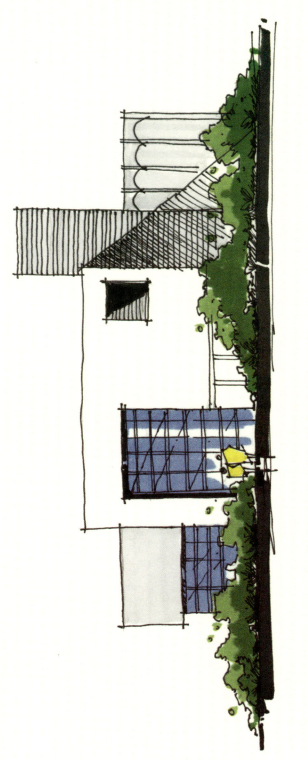

9.20

Exterior elevation plan (marker, ink)

9.22

Interior elevation (marker, ink, colored pencil)

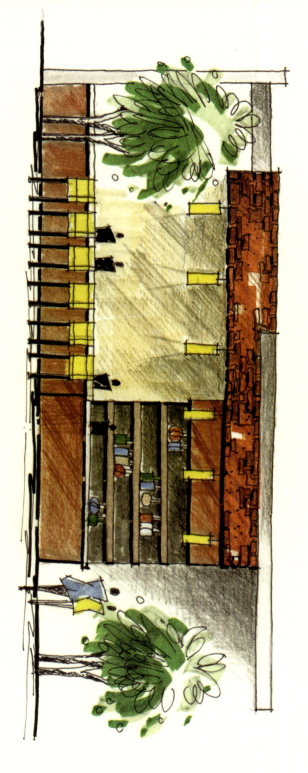

Interior elevation (marker, ink, colored pencil)

9.21

ISOMETRIC VIEW PRESENTATION

Isometric view presentation is also used in schematic design. It is a method that presents design concepts effectively and clearly. It looks like perspective, but it is simpler. Isometric views can present three-dimensional spatial relationships clearly. Using markers and inks, you can create professional-looking isometric views quickly.

The following is the procedure for creating an isometric drawing:

1. Use pencil to sketch the isometric view of a space. You also can add a few trees in the space in order to make the drawing look more playful.

2. Use lighter markers to render areas with different materials.

3. Use colored pencils to create texture for different materials, such as marble or wood.

4. Use a fine-tip marker (Prismacolor brand) to draw some 45-degree strokes in order to add some textures and more values. You also can use colored pencils to achieve these effects.

5. Use a darker marker or a Sharpie to create shadows at recessed areas, such as underneath the furniture, in order to create contrast.

6. Use an Ultra Fine Point Sharpie to trace the pencil lines. Pay attention to line qualities, such as skip lines or dashed lines.

7. Use marker to render tree elevation views. Once again, you do not need to color the entire tree. Leave some white showing. Use black, thick Sharpies to draw shadows.

Figures 9.23 and 9.24 are examples of isometric view presentations with markers, colored pencils, and Sharpies.

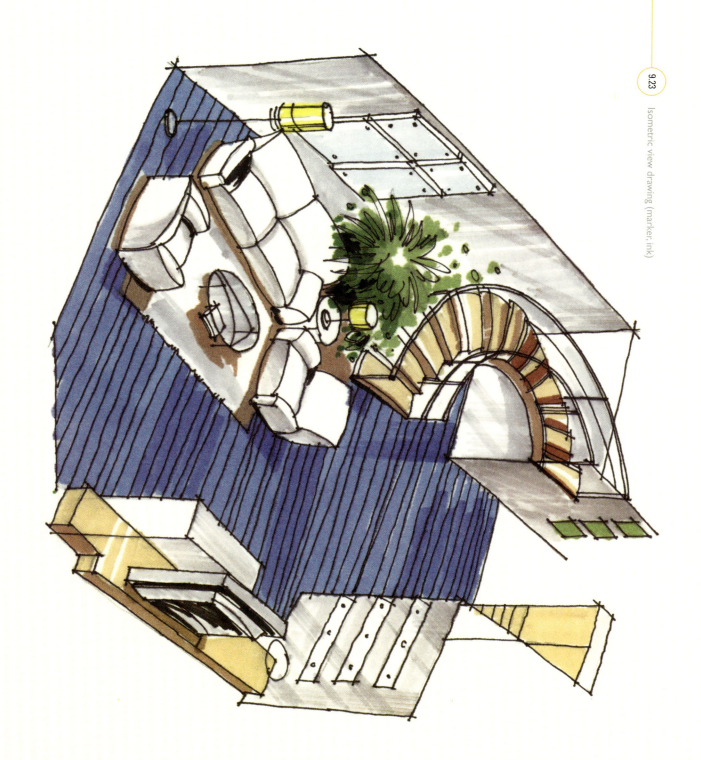

Isometric view drawing (marker, ink)

Isometric view drawing (marker, ink, colored pencil)

9.24

PERSPECTIVE PRESENTATION

Perspective presentation is one of the most popular methods of presenting design concepts. Interior designers and architects use both interior and exterior perspective to convey their design intent. In schematic design, using markers and inks are an effective way to create perspectives quickly. An accurate perspective is essential, even though minor mistakes and imperfections are unavoidable due to the nature of mind-hand coordination. Figures 9.25 and 9.26 are examples of perspective presentations with markers and ink, as well as colored pencils.

The following is the procedure for creating interior perspective:

1. Use pencil to sketch interior perspective including all the details, such as caseworks, furniture, and even accessories. You also can add a few trees or some human figures in order to present a sense of scale and proportion.

2. Use lighter markers to render areas with different materials.

3. Combine markers with colored pencils to create texture for different materials, such as stone or marble. You do not need to draw every single piece of stone or brick.

9.25
Interior perspective drawing (marker, ink)

4. Use fine-tip marker (Prismacolor brand) to draw some 45-degree strokes in order to add some textures and add more values. You also can use colored pencils to achieve these effects.

5. Use a darker marker or Sharpie to create shadows at recessed areas, such as a niche, in order to make the drawing look three-dimensional.

6. Use an Ultra Fine Point Sharpie to trace the pencil lines. Pay attention to line qualities, such as skip lines or dashed lines.

7. Use markers to render tree elevation views. You do not need to color the entire tree. Leave some white showing. Use black, thick Sharpies to draw shadows (Figure 9.25).

8. Use markers to add color to human figures. Usually the human figures are added at the place where viewers' attention is drawn, such as the focal point or entrance. The colors selected usually are very bright.

The objective of this exercise is to get familiar with tree drawings because they are a very important component in plan and elevation presentations.

You may use your marker paper to trace the plan view trees and tree elevations in this chapter. Then you can draw plan view trees and tree elevations in your sketchbook with Sharpies.

The objective of this exercise is to get familiar with floor plan rendering using markers and Sharpies. You should utilize the skills that you learned in previous chapters, such as material presentation, when you render the floor plan. Showing different materials on the floor plan will add more detail to your drawing, thus making it look much more polished.

You can use any drawing, such as an AutoCAD drawing, as a base. First, trace the floor plan on the marker paper. Then use markers to render the floor plan. Finally, use ink to finish up the drawing.

EXERCISE

PRACTICING FLOOR PLAN
RENDERING WITH MARKERS AND INK

9.2

EXERCISE 9.3

PRACTICING ELEVATION RENDERING WITH MARKERS AND INK

The objective of this exercise is to get familiar with elevation rendering using markers and ink. You should utilize the skills that you learned in previous chapters, such as material presentation and tree elevations. A nice tree elevation will add vitality to your drawing.

You can use a drawing, such as an AutoCAD drawing, as a base. First, trace the elevation on the marker paper. Then use markers to render the elevation. Finally, use ink to finish up the drawing.

A good and accurate perspective can make your design look better and more appealing to your client. This exercise will help you to create attractive perspective with markers and ink.

Choose one of your favorite interior space photos from a book or magazine. Sketch the interior space with accurate perspective. Use markers and ink to render it. You may want to use colored pencils to add some final touches.

EXERCISE

PRACTICING PERSPECTIVE RENDERING WITH MARKERS AND INK

9.4

SUMMARY

In this chapter, you:

- Were introduced to tree presentations with ink (plan view and elevation).

- Were introduced to tree rendering using markers and Sharpies.

- Have rendered two-dimensional presentations (floor plan and elevation) with markers and ink.

- Learned how to create three-dimensional presentations (isometric view and perspective) with markers and ink by using the examples provided.

- Learned how to add entourage to your drawings.

Presentation skill is very important for designers. The more practice you have the better you will be. Keep practicing!

KEY TERMS

Car Presentation	Entourage	Human Figure	Perspective
Elevation	Floor Plan	Isometric View	Tree Presentation

1. Isometric presentation is easier compared with perspective. Mastering isometric presentation will add more to your presentation skills. Isometric drawing presents spatial relationship clearly. Figure 9.27 is an isometric drawing. Use marker paper and pencil to trace the floor plan. Then use markers and Sharpies to present materials and finish it up. If you are able to create an isometric drawing by yourself, use your floor plan and elevation as you desire to create an isometric view. Then render the isometric view with markers and ink.

2. The objective of this exercise (Figure 9.28) is to practice floor plan rendering with markers and Sharpies. You also need to add the landscaping at the entrance as shown in Figures 9.16 and 9.17.

ADDITIONAL EXERCISES

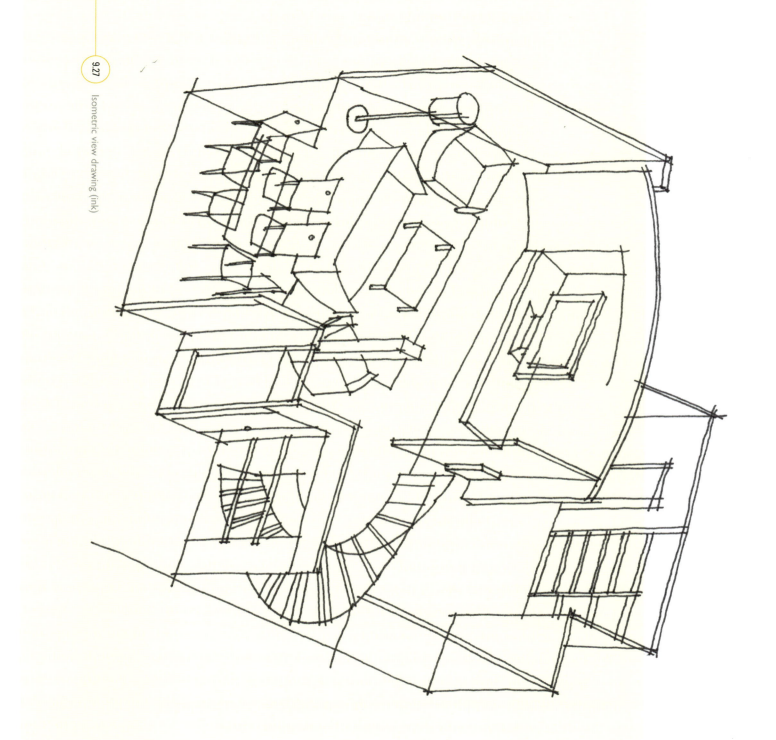

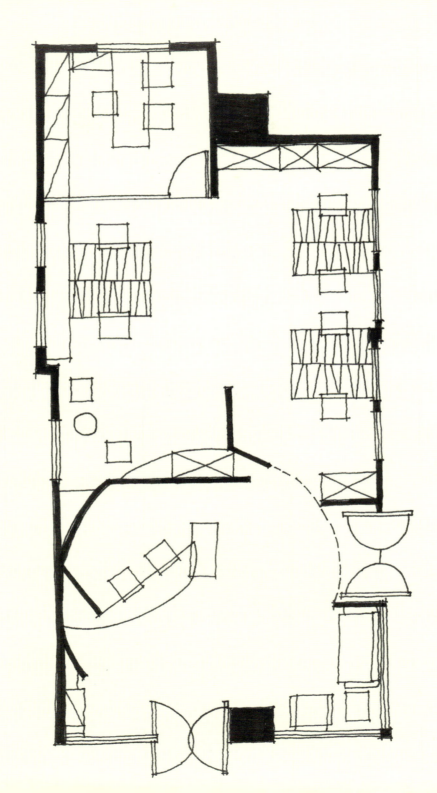

Floor plan (ink)

9.28

10

TRANSFORMING HAND DRAWINGS TO DIGITAL DRAWINGS

CHARACTERISTICS OF FREEHAND SKETCHING

There is consensus among designers that in the creative working process, freehand lines and graphics are infinitely superior to mechanically engineered lines and forms— especially early on in that partially understood, partially sensed stage where designers explore possible and alternative solutions of design problems. This is because the freehand line suggests a uniquely individual human thought-and-action partnership.

Freehand sketching is an example of a phenomenon often referred to as eye– mind–hand coordination. Lines made in this way are not "perfect." Designers, architects, or artists are all aware of these particular imperfections, the way such marks subtly document a level of craft and a state of mind as "human." The lines may be wobbly or wander aimlessly. All these imperfections are the characteristics of freehand sketching. These imperfect lines and strokes all come directly from designers. People recognize the human attributes and personalities present in freehand lines, marks, and strokes.

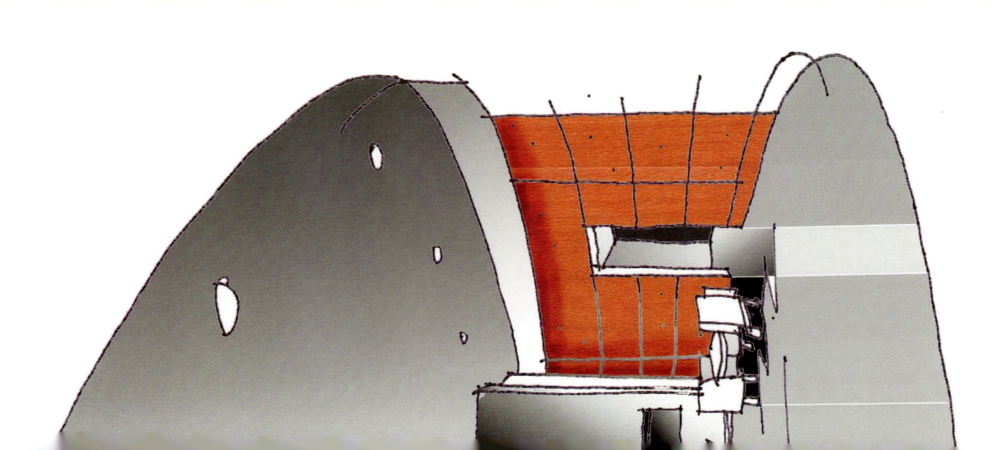

TRANSFORMING FREEHAND TO DIGITAL

Although the computer is an increasingly powerful tool for constructing, rendering, and animating three-dimensional models and can even generate geometries that are beyond human ability, it cannot reveal or clarify the state of mind where individuality and creativity takes place. It does not really matter if mechanically engineered lines are drafted by triangle and T-square or by computer-aided design software. It does matter that the drawings present the designer's personality and immediate response of solving problems. Mechanically created images seem absent of all evidence of human spirit and passion. Thus, keeping freehand sketching in the schematic design phase, and representing the characteristics of freehand drawing is crucial for designers in the design process.

Figures 10.1 through 10.4 are interior perspective drawings that have been transformed from freehand drawings to digital drawings with Photoshop. In these ink drawings, you can see the characteristics of typical freehand drawings. They are free and loose. You can feel the human touch through these freehand lines in transformed digital drawings.

Procedures for Transformation from Freehand to Digital

The first step in the process is to create freehand line drawings, such as floor plans, interior elevations, perspectives, or isometric drawings. The second step is to scan the line drawings into PDF or EPS files. You can search the Internet to help find free photos of materials, such as wood flooring, marble countertops, glass walls, and trees or plants. The final step is to use Photoshop to edit the line drawings that are in PDF or EPS format. The following procedures outline the steps for making this transformation as seamless as possible.

STEP ONE: FREEHAND SKETCHING

You can sketch floor plans, interior elevations, perspectives, and isometric views or even sections, as you desire. It is very important to be loose when you sketch. Do not be afraid of mistakes. This is a very critical step for keeping the characteristics of freehand sketching in the digital drawing. Lines made in this way are not "perfect." They may wiggle or wander aimlessly. But these imperfections reveal the original strokes and marks made by hand. These hand-drawn lines also present the personality and style of the designer.

Interior lobby (Photoshop, ink)

10.2

10.4

10.3

Waiting area in interior space (ink)

Waiting area in interior space (Photoshop, ink)

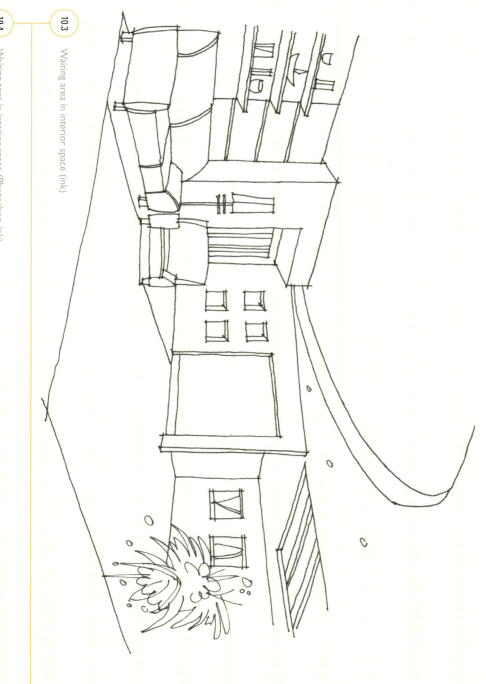

As the mind behind these strokes becomes more confident and engaged, the marks themselves tend to progress from tentative to firm for the design solution. Such lines and shapes record designers' immediate creative thinking. Experienced designers and architects all recognize and appreciate the human attributes present in freehand marks. Therefore, keeping these characteristics is extremely critical.

STEP TWO: TRANSFORMATION FROM FREEHAND TO DIGITAL WITH SCANNING AND INTERNET SEARCH

After your freehand line drawings are created, it is time to transform them into a digital format. A scanner is necessary for this step, to create a PDF or EPS file. Place the drawings on a scanner and scan them to PDF files, as shown in Figures 10.1 and 10.3. You will use these PDF files for Photoshop editing in the next step.

At this time, you also need to find real materials on the Internet to use in your drawings. You can use Google to search images. You also can use recommended links for materials and pattern searches. These sites are free for downloading images.

Figures 10.5 to 10.20 show samples of images used in Photoshop editing. These images were retrieved from Google or recommended links.

1. Floor Materials
  a. Carpet (Figure 10.5)
  b. Marble (Figure 10.6)
  c. Stone Tile (Figure 10.7)
  d. Area Rug (Figure 10.8)

Marble (Photo © Lucy Baldwin/Shutterstock)

10.6

Area rug (Photo © Shutterstock)

10.8

Carpet (Photo © Fedorov Oleksiy/Shutterstock)

10.5

Stone tile (Photo © Konstantnin/Shutterstock)

10.7

Blue marble (Photo © Alexander Kalina/Shutterstock)

10.9

Wood veneer (Photo© Maxim Tupikov/Shutterstock)

10.10

2. Furniture or Countertop Materials
 a. Blue Marble (Figure 10.9)
 b. Wood Veneer (Figure 10.10)
 c. Green Marble (Figure 10.11)
 d. Birch Wood (Figure 10.12)

Green marble (Photo courtesy of http://www.cgtextures.com/ index.php)

10.11

10.12

Birch wood (Photo © Christophe Testi/Shutterstock)

3. Wall Materials
 a. Blue Glass (Figure 10.13)
 b. Textured Glass (Figure 10.14)
 c. Brick (Figure 10.15)
 d. Wood Panel (Figure 10.16)

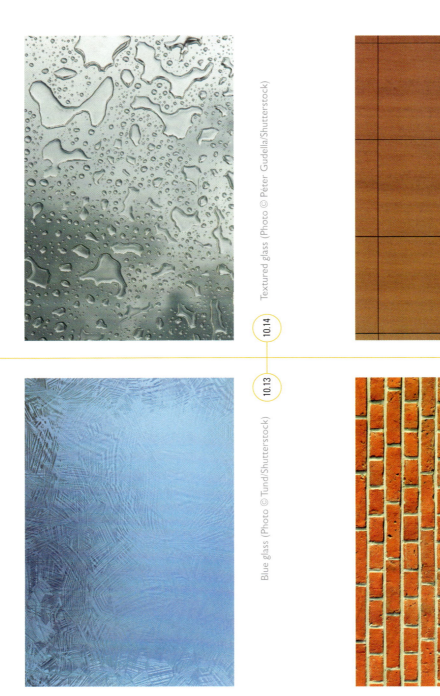

Textured glass (Photo © Péter Gudella/Shutterstock)

10.14

Blue glass (Photo © Tund/Shutterstock)

10.13

Wood panel (Photo courtesy of http://www.cgtextures.com/index.php)

10.16

Brick (Photo © Shutterstock)

10.15

These images were used in the floor plan, interior elevation, perspectives, and isometric drawings in this chapter. You should edit the images as needed in order to present materials with clear textures. You can edit these images in Photoshop by scaling the image or even creating perspective views for the materials, among other options. This process will be explained in the next step.

The following exercises involve creating freehand drawings of floor plans, interior elevations, perspectives, and isometric drawings. Keeping the characteristics of freehand sketching is very important for the first step, as discussed earlier. After finishing these exercises, you will have all the PDF files ready for Photoshop editing.

4. Nature (Grass, Trees)
- **a.** Grass (Figure 10.17)
- **b.** Tree (Figure 10.18)
- **c.** Gravel (Figure 10.19)
- **d.** Bushes (Figure 10.20)

Grass (Photo © Beata Becla/Shutterstock) 10.17

Tree (Photo © Jan Martin Will/Shutterstock) 10.18

Gravel (Photo courtesy of http://www.cgtextures.com/index.php) 10.19

Bushes (Photo © Shutterstock) 10.20

Use your Sharpie and marker paper to trace any floor plans that were drawn previously. Next, scan these interior floor plans into PDF files for further Photoshop editing. The scanned files can also be saved as EPS files. Figures 10.21 and 10.22 are examples for your reference. Figure 10.21 is a PDF file created by scanning a freehand drawing. Figure 10.22 is a transformed digital drawing created by Photoshop. In Figure 10.22, carpet, wood floor, marble floor, and grass images were used in Photoshop. Gradient fills were used on furniture. The Burn tool was used to create shadows underneath the furniture. All these tools in Photoshop will be introduced in detail in the next step.

Figures 10.23 and 10.24 provide an example of creating a digital drawing for a floor plan from an ink sketch (Figure 10.23). Real materials, such as wood floor, marble floor, and carpet were downloaded from the Internet to create the digital version in Figure 10.24. In order to create the contrast and provide a background for the floor plan, the Gradient tool was used for creating background.

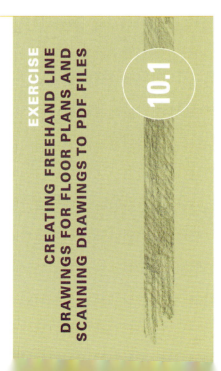

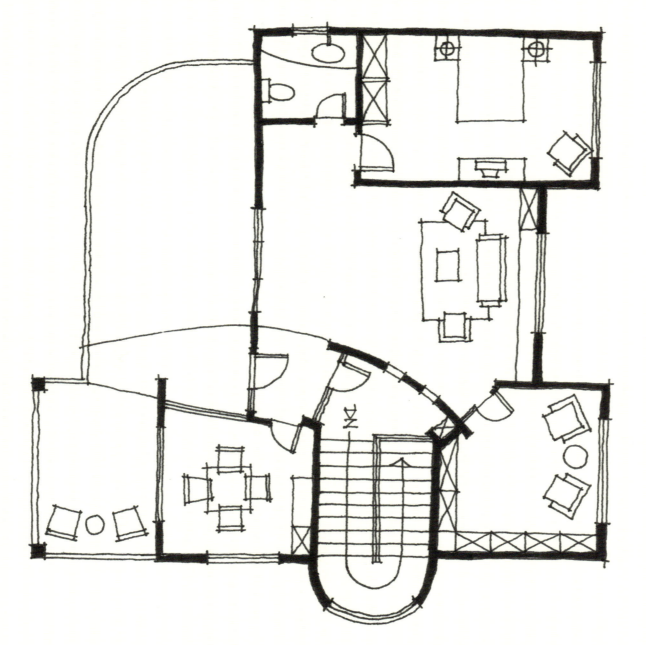

10.21

Residential floor plan (Photoshop, ink)

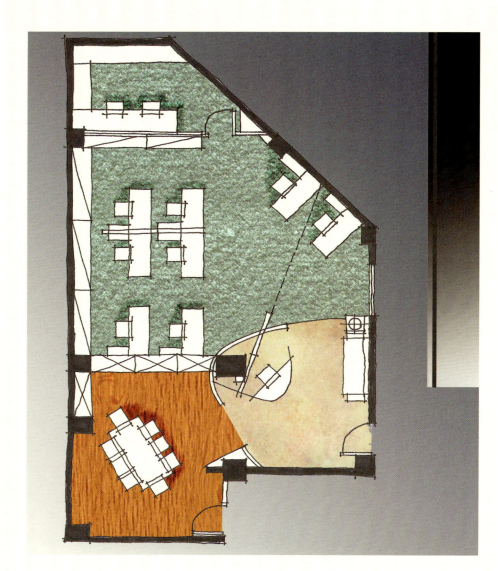

10.24

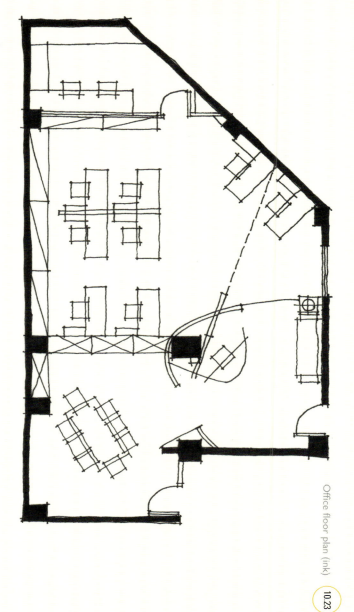

10.23

Use your ink pen and marker paper to trace any interior elevations that were drawn previously. Next, scan these interior elevations into PDF files for further Photoshop editing. Remember to be loose and free when you sketch. This is a very critical step for keeping the characteristics of freehand sketching in digital drawing. In Figure 10.25, freehand lines were used. Trees were rendered with markers. Figure 10.26 shows a transformed digital drawing, with freehand strokes and marks. Figures 10.27 and 10.28 are another pair of drawings showing the transformation from a freehand interior elevation sketch to a digital version.

EXERCISE

CREATING FREEHAND LINE DRAWINGS FOR INTERIOR ELEVATIONS AND SCANNING DRAWINGS TO PDF FILES

10.2

10.26 Interior elevation (Photoshop, ink, marker)

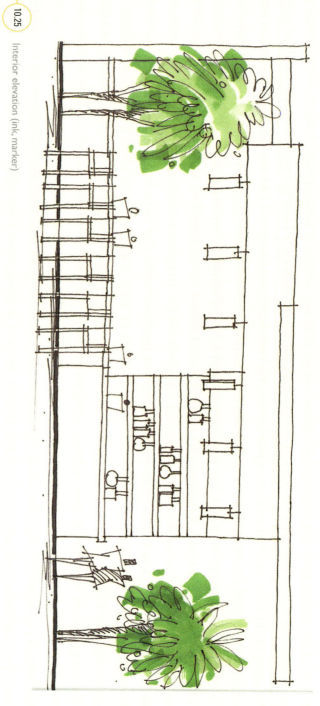

10.25 Interior elevation (ink, marker)

Interior elevation (ink, marker)

Interior elevation (Photoshop, ink, marker)

10. TRANSFORMING HAND DRAWINGS TO DIGITAL DRAWINGS   245

EXERCISE

CREATING FREEHAND LINE
DRAWINGS FOR INTERIOR
PERSPECTIVES AND SCANNING
DRAWINGS TO PDF FILES

10.3

Use your Sharpie and marker paper to trace any interior perspectives that were drawn previously. Next, scan these interior perspectives into PDF or EPS files for further Photoshop editing. Remember to be loose and free when you sketch. In the following two pairs of examples (Figures 10.29 to 10.32), the plants were rendered by marker. It added a human touch and enhanced the characteristics of freehand sketching in a digital format.

10.29

Interior perspective (ink, marker)

10.30

Interior perspective (Photoshop, ink, marker)

Interior perspective (ink, marker)

10.31

Interior perspective (Photoshop, ink, marker)

10.32

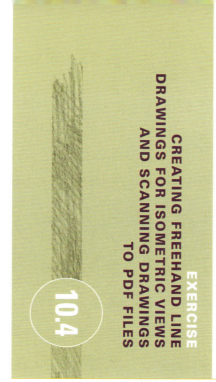

EXERCISE

**CREATING FREEHAND LINE
DRAWINGS FOR ISOMETRIC VIEWS
AND SCANNING DRAWINGS
TO PDF FILES**

10.4

Use your Sharpie and marker paper to trace any isometric views that were drawn previously. Next, scan these isometric drawings into PDF or EPS files for further Photoshop editing. Figure 10.33 is a freehand isometric drawing in ink. Figure 10.34 was edited by Photoshop with real materials, such as wood and marble floor and trees. Figures 10.35 and 10.36 show an isometric view of a residential space in ink and in a digitized version.

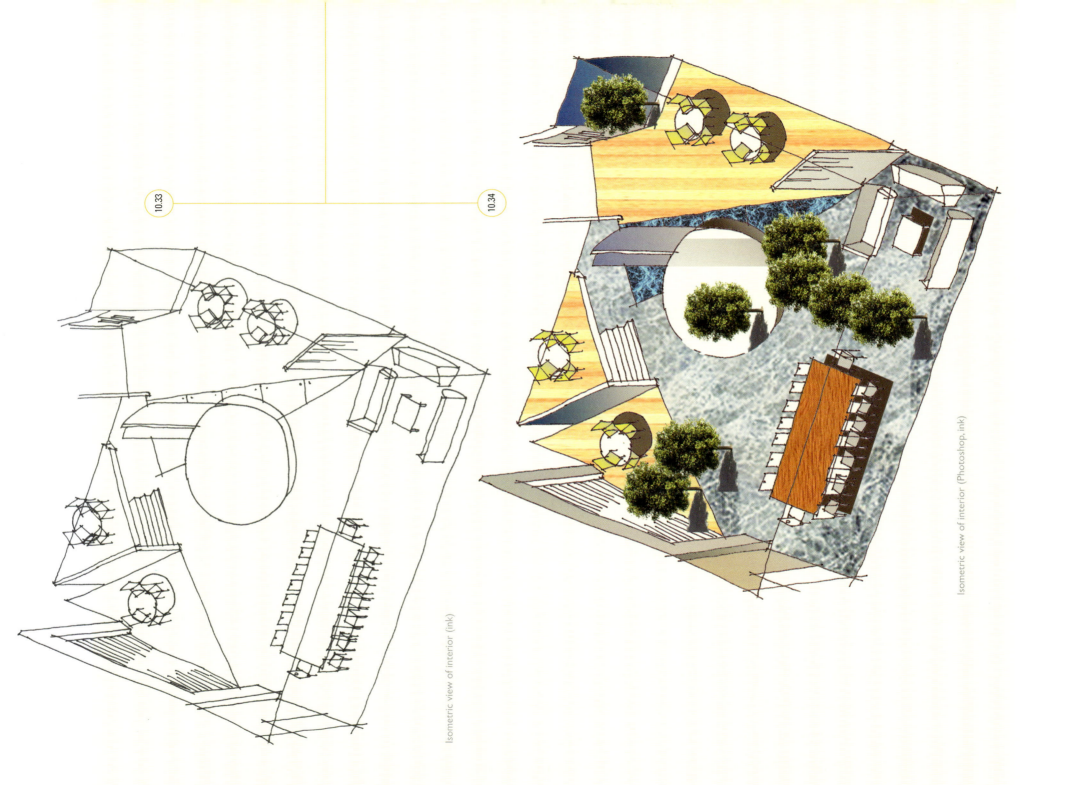

Isometric view of interior (ink)

Isometric view of interior (Photoshop, ink)

Isometric view of residential space (ink)

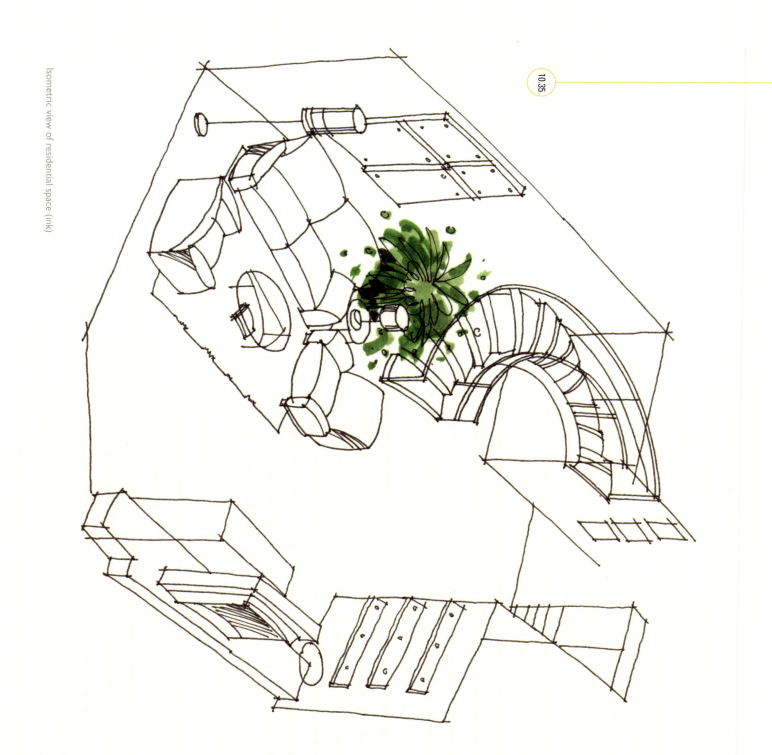

10.35

Isometric view of residential space (Photoshop, ink, marker)

10.36

DIGITAL IMAGE EDITING WITH PHOTOSHOP

As introduced earlier in this chapter, the first step in digital image editing was to create freehand line drawings. These line drawings were then scanned into PDF files. An Internet search was conducted to find photos of real materials to incorporate into the digital drawing. The next step is to use Photoshop to edit the line drawings that are in PDF or EPS format. To be able to use Photoshop is critical in order to transform drawings. Therefore, the following steps will walk you through some of the fundamental tools used in Photoshop. The intention is to help you become familiar with Photoshop before introducing more detailed procedures. The procedures described are generic to the Photoshop platform in order to accommodate different versions of the program.

BRIEF INTRODUCTION OF PHOTOSHOP

By using Photoshop, you will be able to edit freehand drawings and include simulations of real materials, patterns or solids, and gradient fills. Therefore, mastering Photoshop software is very important in the transformation process of creating very polished presentation designs. All the basic features of Photoshop can be learned from the following introduction. Additional learning material is available from Photoshop manuals. Additionally, when you are working in Photoshop, you always have access to an online Help menu. You can access the Help menu by clicking on Help on the toolbar on top of your screen.

Figure 10.37 shows the screen when you first open Photoshop. At the top of your screen is a toolbar that contains the File, Edit, Image, Layer, Select, Filter, View, Window, and Help pull-down menus.

Figure 10.38 shows the Help pull-down menu, which allows you to access the Photoshop Help menu. After you click on that option, you can then click on a Search link. Then you will be prompted with a new screen, which allows you to type in the key words that you want to search, for example, "crop drawing."

Figure 10.39 presents the Rectangular Marquee tool as a default, which allows you to select objects. Normally, you just need to cross window, which means clicking on the screen with the upper left corner of the rectangle and drag your mouse. Next, click on the lower right corner of the rectangle in order to select the object.

Select the appropriate Marquee tool for your purpose; the following two Marquees tools are used often.

- Rectangular Marquee  to make a rectangular selection.

- Elliptical Marquee to make an elliptical selection.

10.37   Opening Photoshop

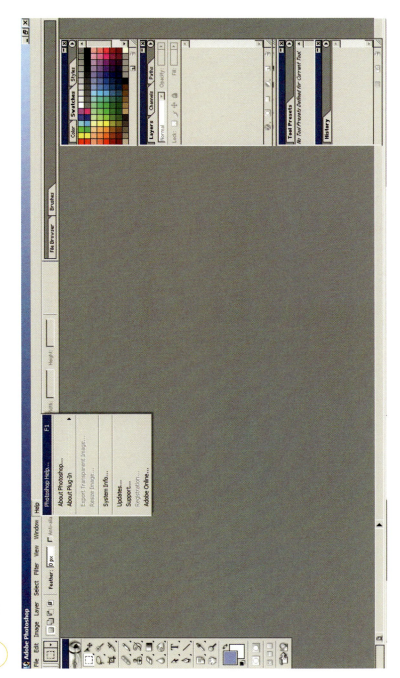

10.38 Help pull-down menu

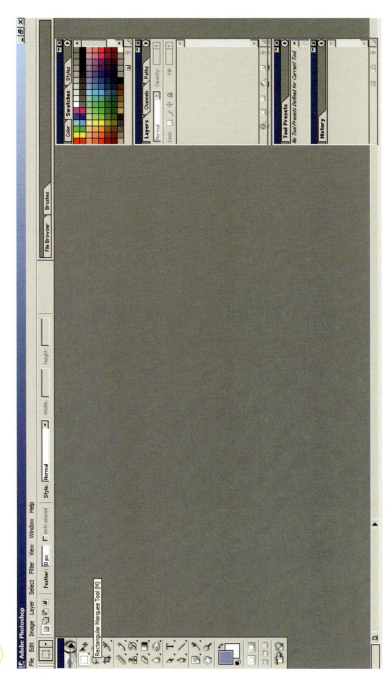

10.39 Rectangular Marquee tool

Figure 10.40 shows the Move tool, which allows you to move the object. When you need to move an object, you need to make sure that the layer is current or active. To make the layer active, click on the layer name on the right side of your screen. The function of the layers is allowing you to add content to them. For example, you can create a layer called "furniture." Then you can draw

furniture on that layer by making it current. The layer function organizes all the objects you created by each individual layer. You can create as many layers as you want.

Figure 10.41 shows a Magic Wand tool, which allows you to select a color area (for example, a blue marble tabletop) without having to trace its outline. By using the Magic Wand, you can select the object with

a closed boundary, you cannot use the Magic Wand tool on an image in Bitmap mode.

Cropping is the process of removing portions of an image to create focus or strengthen the composition. Figure 10.42 shows a Crop tool, which allows you to crop your drawing—make your drawing smaller—so that selected objects can become a focal point.

10.40

Move tool

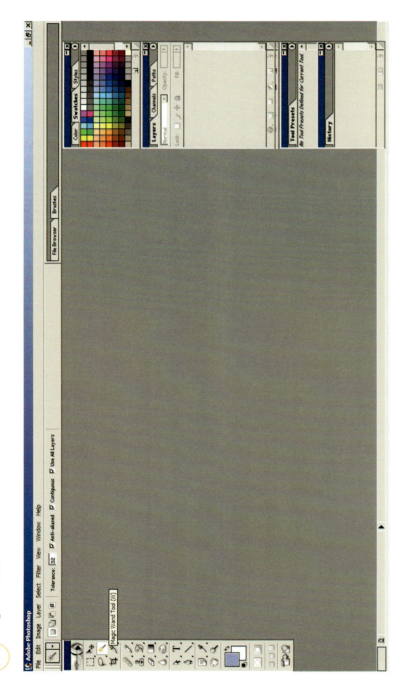

10.41   Magic Wand tool

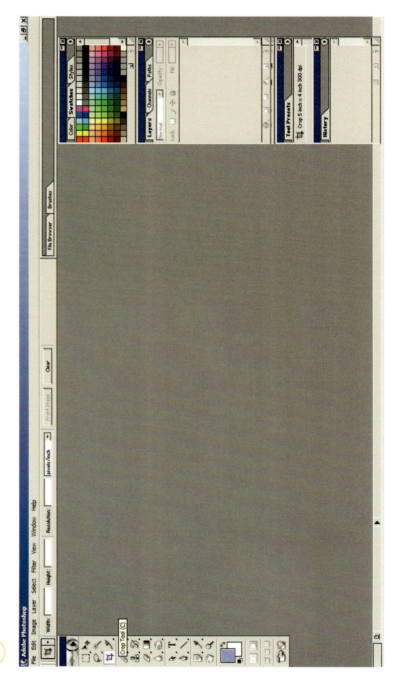

10.42   Crop tool

The Clone Stamp tool takes a sample of an image, which you can then apply over another image or part of the same image. Figure 10.43 shows the Clone Stamp tool, which allows you to duplicate the image.

Figure 10.44 shows where you can find the Eraser, which allows you to erase unwanted lines and drawings. The Eraser tool changes pixels in the image as you drag through them.

The Gradient tool creates a gradient blend between multiple colors. There are several different gradient fills, such as linear gradient and angle gradient. The linear gradient is used to shade from the starting point to the ending point in a straight line. The angle gradient is used to shade in a counterclockwise sweep around the starting point. These two gradients are used often, especially in the

transformation process. Figure 10.45 shows where you can find the Gradient tool and the Paint Bucket tool, which allows you to fill in with gradient fill or solid fill. The Paint Bucket tool fills adjacent pixels that are similar in color value to color swatches that you click on in the palette shown on the right-hand side of the screen.

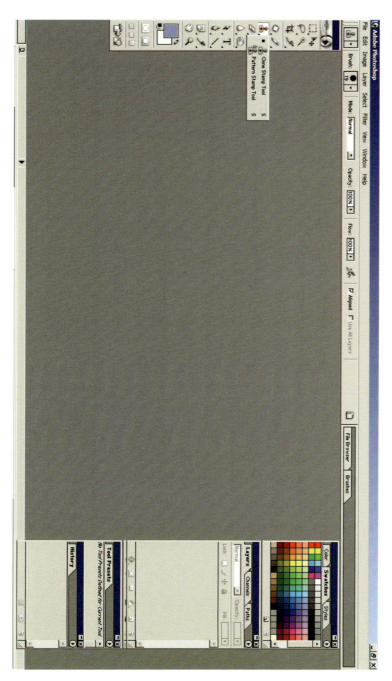

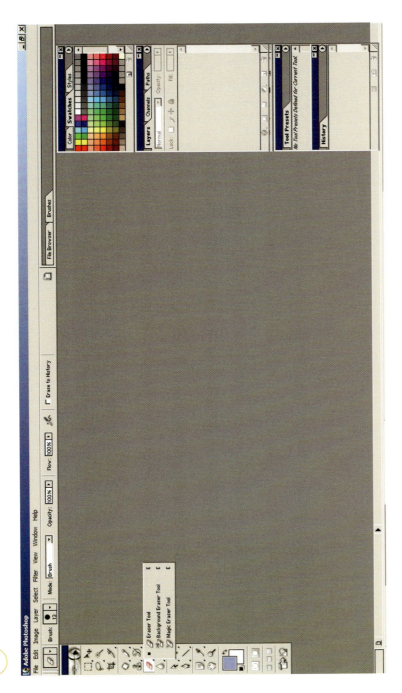

10.44 Eraser tool

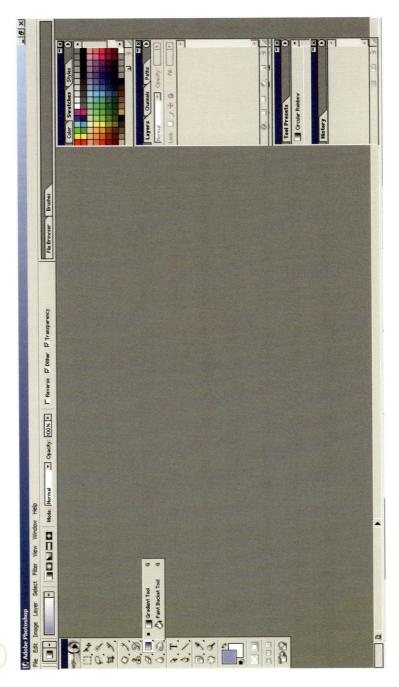

10.45 Gradient tool and Paint Bucket tool

The toning tools consist of the Dodge tool and the Burn tool, which are used to lighten or darken the areas of the image. Figure 10.46 shows where you can find the Dodge tool and Burn tool. The Dodge tool allows you to make the area lighter, while the Burn tool allows you to create shadows or make the area darker.

1. Select the Dodge tool ✎ or the Burn tool ✋.

2. Do the following in the options bar, which is located on the top of screen:

- Choose a brush and set brush options.

- In the Range drop-down menu, select what to change in the image: Midtones to change the middle range of grays; Shadows to change the dark areas; Highlights to change the light areas.

- Specify the Exposure for the tool. Exposure can range from 1 to 100 percent. For transparent paint or a weak effect, specify a low percentage value; for more opaque paint or a strong effect, specify a high value.

- Click the Airbrush button ✎ on the horizontal toolbar to use the brush as an airbrush. Alternately, select the Airbrush option in the Brushes palette.

3. Drag the brush over the part of the image you want to modify.

Figure 10.47 shows where you can find the Line tool. You can use the Line tool to draw lines to create a closed boundary when you need to use the Gradient tool or the Paint Bucket tool. You also can use the Line tool to draw lines to create a closed boundary for a gradient or solid background. Therefore, the Line tool is very useful during the transformation process.

The Eyedropper tool samples color to designate a new foreground or background color. Figure 10.48 shows where you can find the Eyedropper tool. You can use the Eyedropper tool to select a color from the Swatches palette.

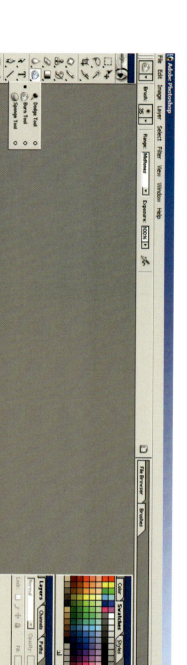

10.46   Dodge tool and Burn tool

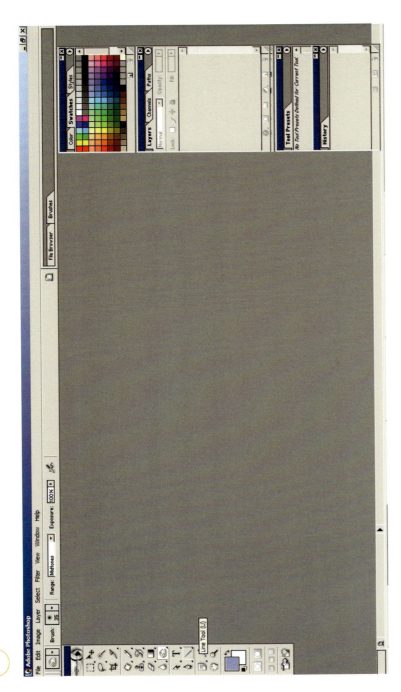

10.47 Line tool

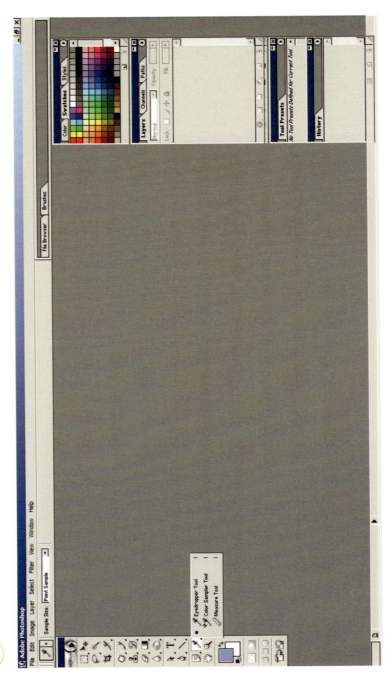

10.48 Eyedropper tool

Figures 10.49 and 10.50 show all the layers on the right side of your screen. When you need to make changes, you need to make that layer active or current by clicking on the layer name. For instance, the blue color highlights the active layer "glass." In

the layers palette as shown in Figure 10.50, the display orders can be changed. You can move another layer above the selected layer. When you create a new layer, it appears either above the selected layer or within the selected layer in the layer palette.

Figure 10.51 shows the color swatches. You can use the Eyedropper tool to select a foreground or background color from the Swatches palette. You also can select the color from the Swatches palette and then use the Gradient tool or the Paint Bucket tool to create gradient fill or solid fill.

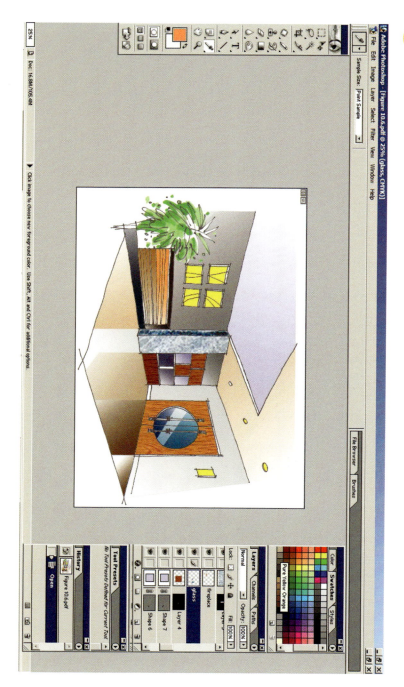

10.49

Activating layers in Layer Palette on the right side of the screen

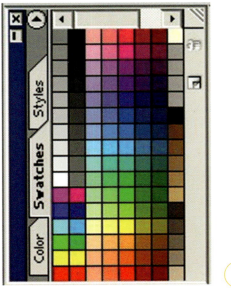

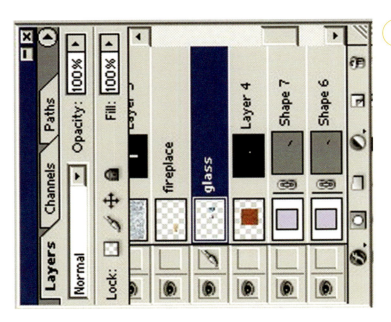

10.50

Blue color highlights the active layer "glass" in Layer Palette

10.51

Color swatches

Procedures for Image Editing with Photoshop

After a freehand sketch has been scanned into PDF format, it is time to start editing your drawing with Photoshop. The editing process is not hard as long as you become familiar with and practice using Photoshop. The edited drawings look very sophisticated compared to freehand drawings. The following steps describe the procedure for creating a final digital drawing in Photoshop.

1. Open up Photoshop and then always open a new file, as shown in Figure 10.52.

2. Set Resolution to 300; choose CMYK color, Letter, and White in contents section. (See Figure 10.53.) Click OK. Then a screen showing a new file in Photoshop will open (Figure 10.54).

3. Go to the File pull-down menu to find Place and click on it. It is shown in Figure 10.55.

10.52 Open a New file

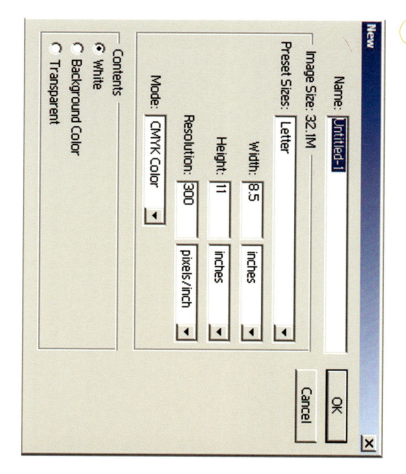

10.53 Set resolution and other parameters

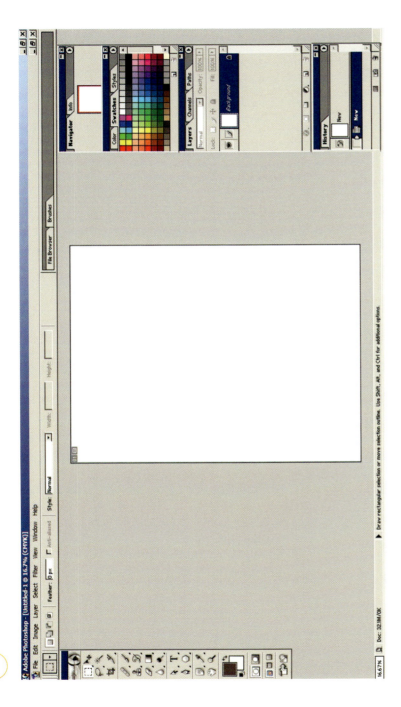

10.54 New file

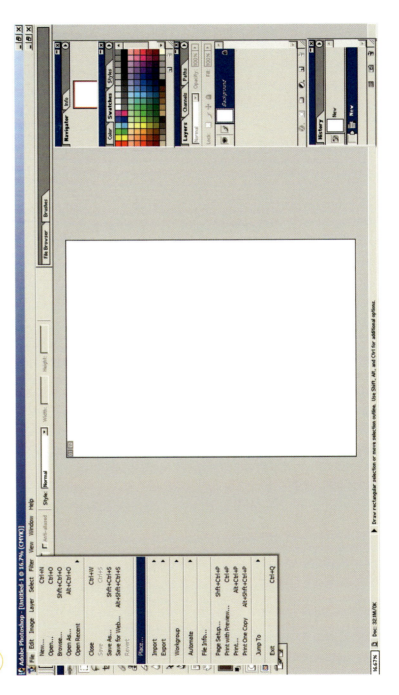

10.55 Click on Place

continued

4. After clicking on Place, you will be prompted by a dialogue box that allows you to browse the PDF file that you have made from your freehand sketch (Figure 10.56). Choose the PDF file, such as Figure 10.1 or 10.3.

5. After you choose your PDF file, you will see a big X on top of the sketch when it appears on the screen (Figure 10.57). To remove the X, just hit the Return key.

6. You need to rename the layer to be used as background. You can rename it as "line drawing" (Figure 10.58).

7. At the little drop-down menu for layers on the right of the screen, change Normal to Multiply and lock it (Figure 10.59). To lock a layer, simply highlight the layer you want to lock and then click on the Lock icon on top of the Layer palette. After you lock a layer, the Lock icon will appear after the layer's name. By locking a layer, you will not be able to make any changes on the objects that are in the locked layer.

10.56   Chose PDF file of sketch

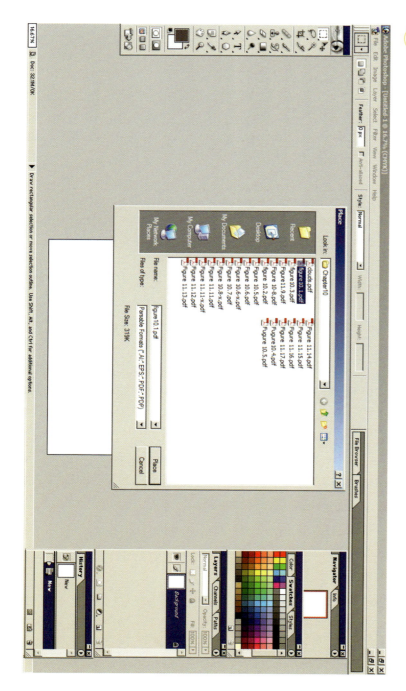

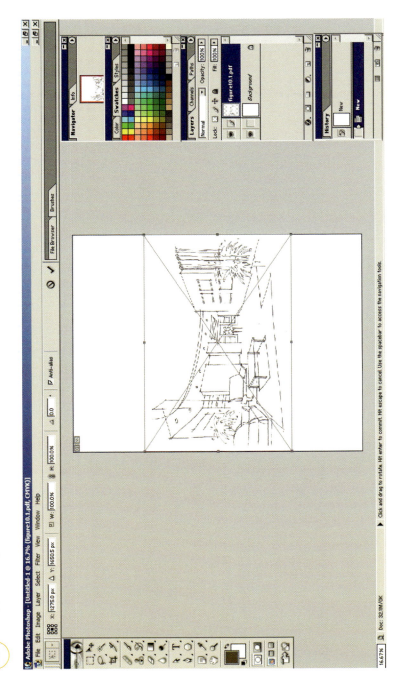

10.57 Hit the Return key to remove the X

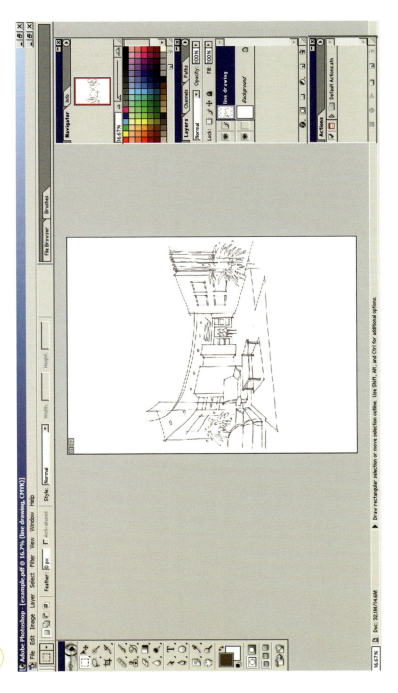

10.58 Rename background layer as "line drawing"

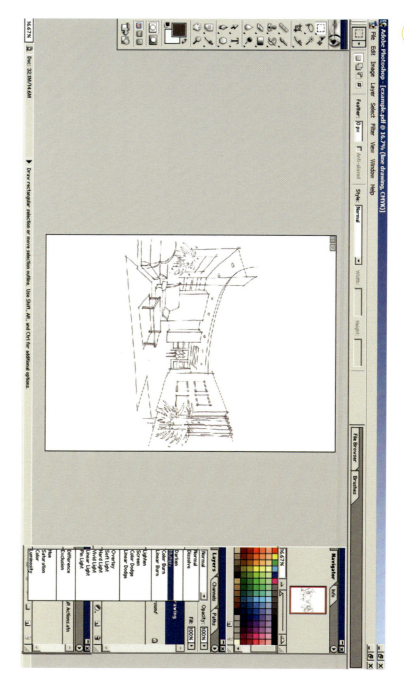

continued

8. To attach real material, such as an image of a marble floor to your PDF file, go to File—then open—marble.jpg in Photoshop as shown in Figure 10.60.

9. Select Marble image with the selection tool (the Rectangular Marquee tool, which is the square with dashed lines as sides on the left side of the screen). Then cross window on the blue marble image (Figure 10.61).

10. If you need to deactivate the selection command, click Ctrl D.

11. Go to the Edit pull-down menu and click on Copy. (Figure 10.61)

12. Switch to your line-drawing PDF file. Use the Magic Wand to select the area that you want to fill in with real material (Figure 10.62). By holding down the Shift key between your selections, you will be able to add new areas of selections to the previous set. In Figure 10.62, the coffee table top was selected.

13. Then use the Paste Into command (*not* Paste) to attach real material to the area that you just specified (Figure 10.63).

14. It is important that you create a new layer for each different material attachment. Figure 10.64 presents the layer "table top."

15. You also can change texture size for the material. Use the selection tool first. Then go to the Edit pull-down menu and use Transform. You can scale, rotate, or create perspective for the material. Figure 10.65 shows a brick material in Photoshop. Figure 10.66 shows the perspective of the material in Photoshop.

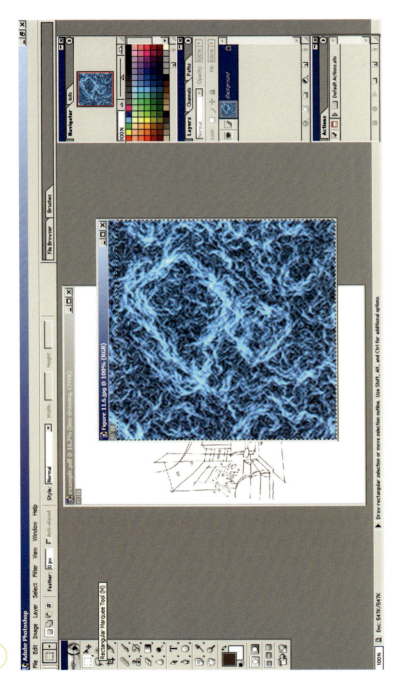

10.60   Add image of real material to the PDF file

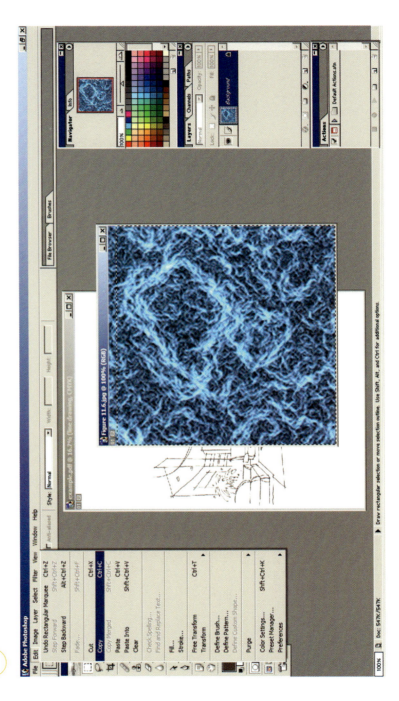

10.61   Select marble image with Rectangular Marquee tool

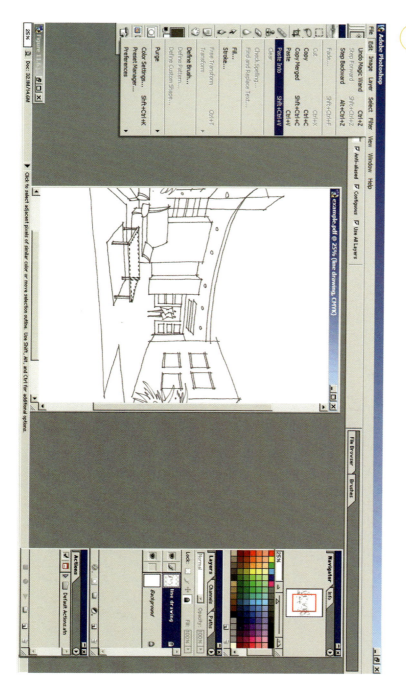

10.63 Use Paste Into command

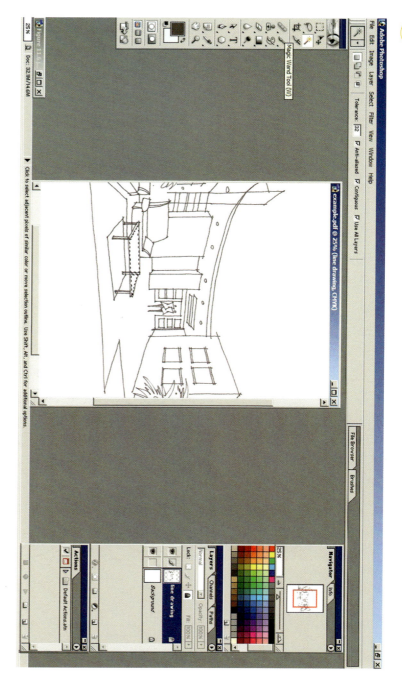

10.62 Use the Magic Wand tool to select an area to fill in with real material

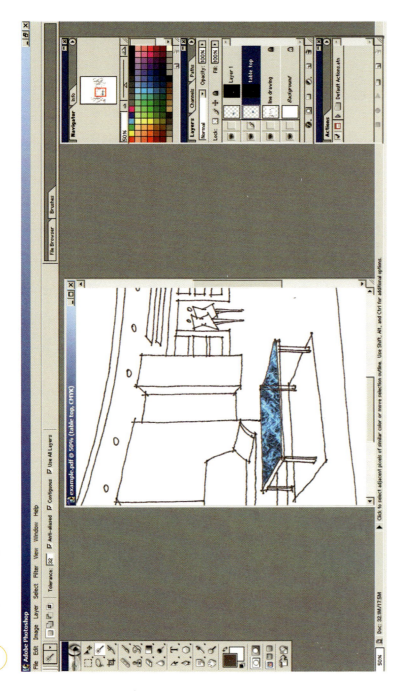

10.64   The layer "table top"

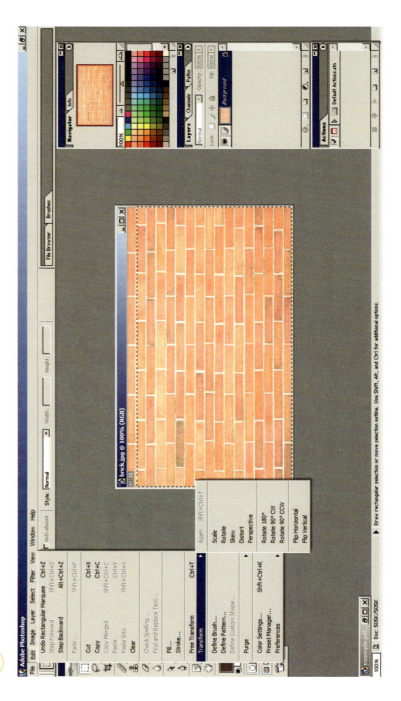

10.65   Use Transform to change texture size

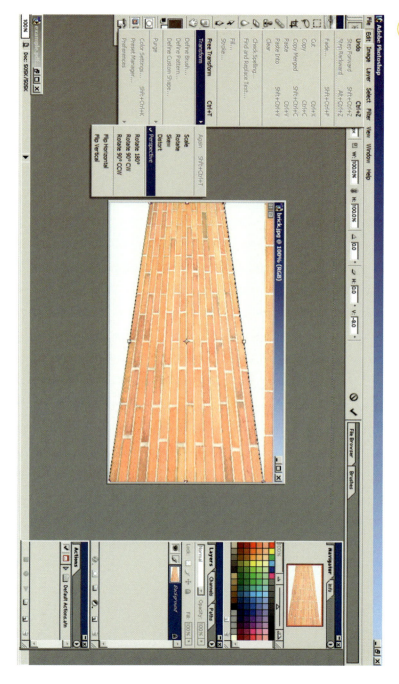

continued

16. For a solid area, you can use the Gradient tool or the Paint Bucket tool to add desired color (Figure 10.67).

17. To create shadow or to make a certain area darker, you can use the Burn tool, which is located below the Paint Bucket tool (Figure 10.68). To make the area lighter, you can use the Dodge tool.

18. To place trees or bushes in your PDF file, you can use Copy and Paste. One important step that you need to do is to remove the background behind the tree. In order to do that, you can use the Magic Wand to select the tree. Then the boundary will be highlighted. Use the Crop command, which can be found in the Image pull-down menu, to remove the background.

19. One special note of caution about this process. If the boundary is not closed, it will not allow you to use the Magic Wand to select the desired area. Therefore, sometimes you will have to draw lines to close the boundary in order to use the Magic Wand.

In addition to the generic procedure of transforming freehand drawings to digital ones as just described, the following section introduces special techniques that will make your drawings more polished. These techniques use photos as background, add shadows, and create entourage, such as human figures and cars. The following example will walk you through the process of bringing a photo in as background, creating entourage, and adding shadows in your drawing.

10.67   Use Gradient tool or Paint Bucket tool for a solid area

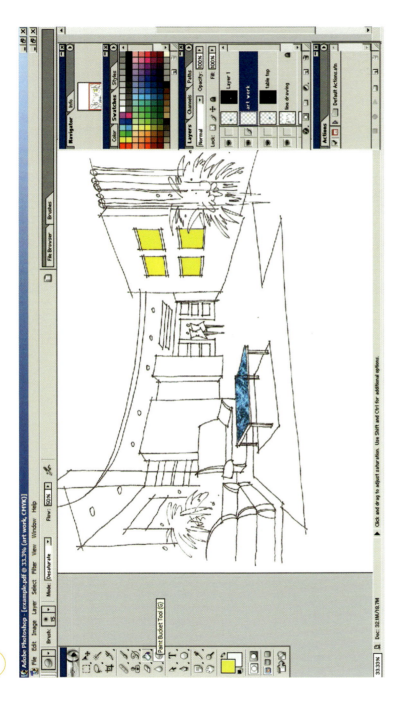

10.68   Location of Burn tool for making area darker

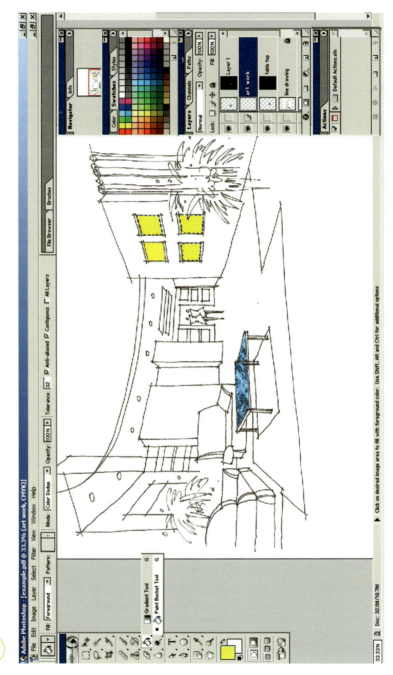

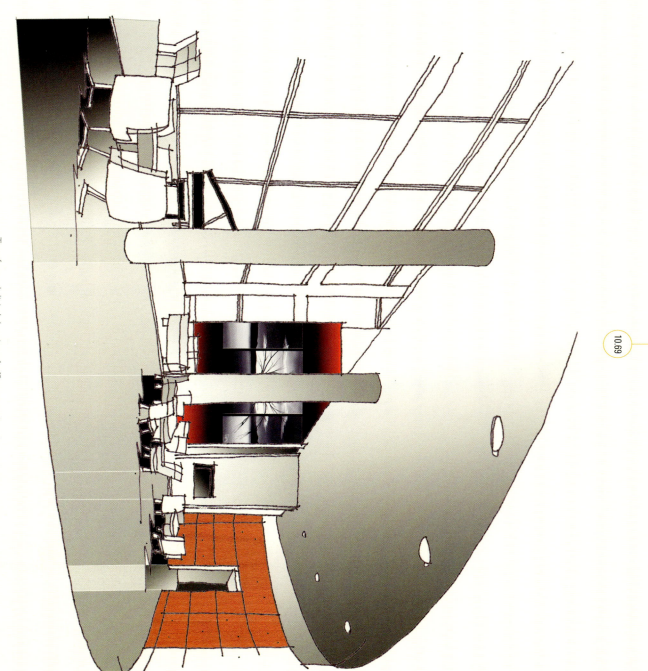

Transformed digital drawing of office space interior

10.69

USING PHOTOS AS BACKGROUND

Figure 10.69 is an interior perspective of lobby area. Wood material was applied on the wall. An abstract painting was also applied on the wall as a mural by using Copy and Paste commands. Gradient fill was used many times for walls, ceiling, and floor as well as furniture. Since it is a building in a city setting, the background photo chosen was a cityscape, as shown in Figure 10.70.

1. Make your background photo with less contrast and lighter because you want to focus on your interior space. Open up your background photo in Photoshop. Go to the Image pull-down menu. Select Adjustments and Brightness/Contrast as shown in Figure 10.71. Then you will be prompted by a dialogue box as shown in Figure 10.72. Make the drawing brighter with less contrast. Your background photo should look like Figure 10.70.

2. Make your background photo's perspective match your interior perspective by using Transform in the Edit pull-down menu. Do not forget to use the Rectangular Marquee tool to select your photo before you select Transform.

3. Use the Magic Wand to select each window panel. You need to hold the shift key down in order to have multiple selections at the same time.

4. Use Copy and Paste Into to complete the process (Figure 10.73). Remember not to use Paste.

 10.70   Cityscape background photo

Make the drawing brighter with less contrast

10.72

Select Adjustments and Brightness/Contrast

10.71

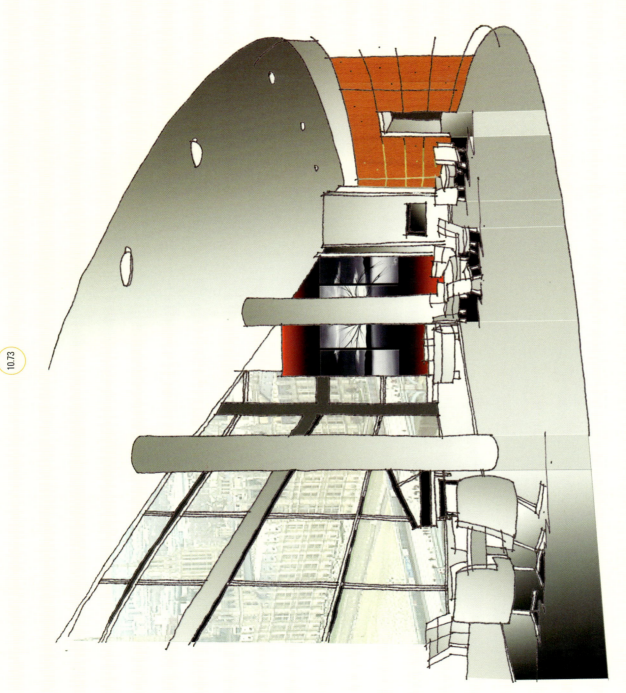

10.73

Use Copy and Paste Into to add your background photo

ADDING ENTOURAGE TO DRAWINGS

It is very common to add entourage to architectural drawings. The entourage, such as people or cars, will present a relative scale for the space. You can use your own photos or download a photo from the Internet. You can use Photoshop to create your own entourage.

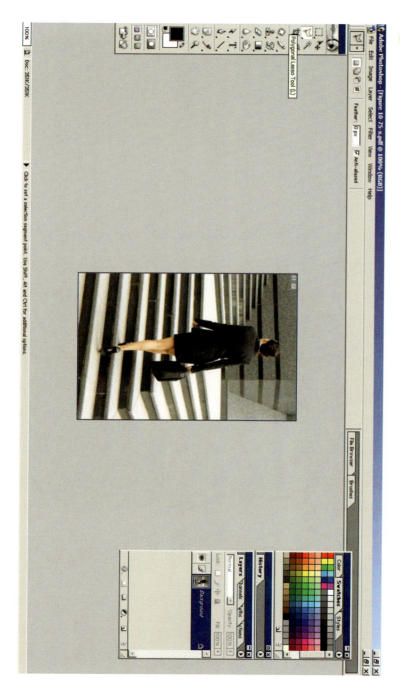

10.74

Select the Polygonal Lasso tool, and trace the edge of a person

1. Open up your photo in Photoshop. Select the Polygonal Lasso tool, and trace the edge of the person or object (Figure 10.74). Next, open up a new file. Copy the selection and paste it to the new file. Save the file with a different name. You can save the file as PDF or EPS to maintain the object without the background (Figures 10.75 and 10.76).

2. Use Transform in the Edit pull-down menu to scale the human figure. Keep in mind the effect of perspective. The person who is closer to the viewer will be bigger than the person who is farther away from the viewer. Figure 10.77 shows two people in different views. The white figure is bigger than the black figure because of the effect of perspective. After you properly scale the figures, you can use Copy and Paste to bring the entourage into your drawing.

3. Use the Move tool to locate the image in the desired location in your drawing.

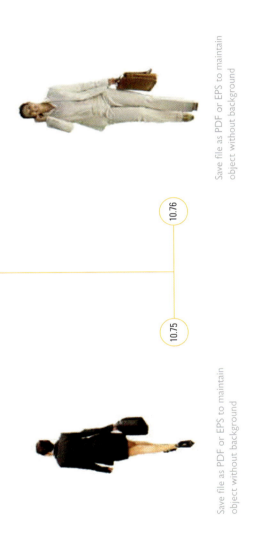

Save file as PDF or EPS to maintain
object without background

10.76

10.75

Save file as PDF or EPS to maintain
object without background

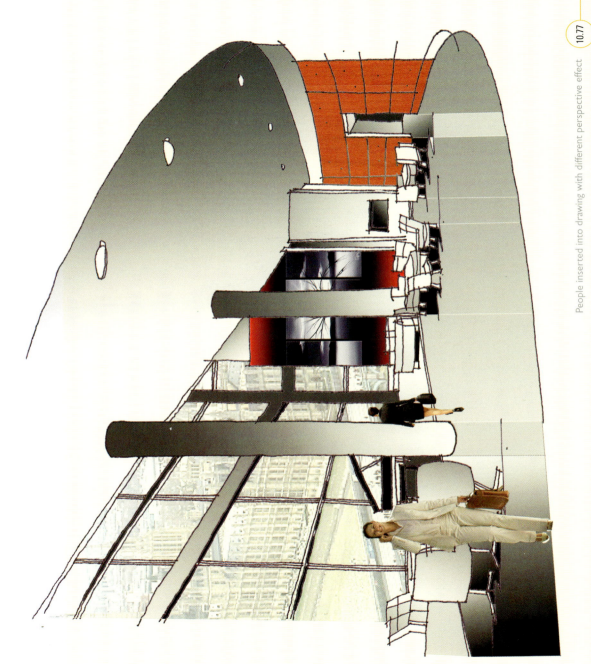

People inserted into drawing with different perspective effect 10.77

ADDING SHADOWS TO DRAWINGS

Adding shadows to your drawing is very important because it creates contrast and adds more interest to the drawing. As introduced earlier in this chapter, you always can use the Burn tool to add value on the object, which means making it darker. You also can add shadows by doing the following:

1. Draw the outline of a person in shadow with the Polygonal Lasso tool. Create a new layer to put the shadow on.

2. Select the Gradient tool from the tool palette.

3. Click and drag the mouse within the selected area to apply the gradient.

4. Adjust the Opacity (located in the Layers palette) of the shadow layer to achieve the desired shadow value

To create a shadow from a person or object, you also can do the following:

1. Open up the person photo in Photoshop. Change the Brightness to a bigger value and change the Contrast to -100, under Image > Adjustments > Brightness/Contrast. See Figure 10.78b.

2. Open up the person photo in Photoshop. Use the Rectangular Marquee tool to select the person in the photo. Then select Edit > Transform > Distort and adjust the size of the shadow to match the person in your drawing.

3. Create a new layer to put the shadow on and make this layer current.

4. Copy the distorted person and Paste it to your drawing. Use the Move tool to bring it to the desired location.

5. Change the Opacity (in the Layers palette) of the shadow to Semitransparent to match the entire drawing (Figure 10.78c).

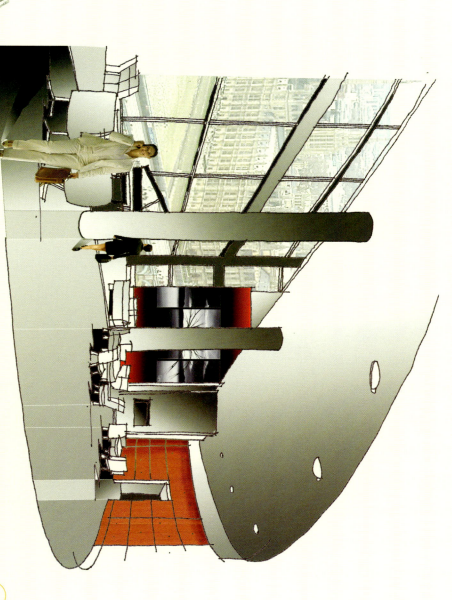

Create the desired shadow value using Gradient tool

10.78a

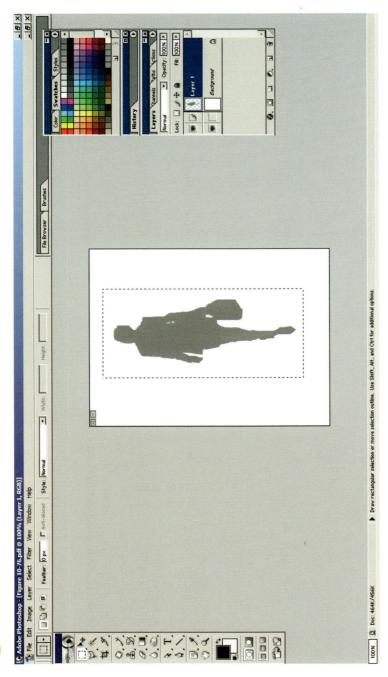

10.78b   Create a shadow from a person or object by using Transform function

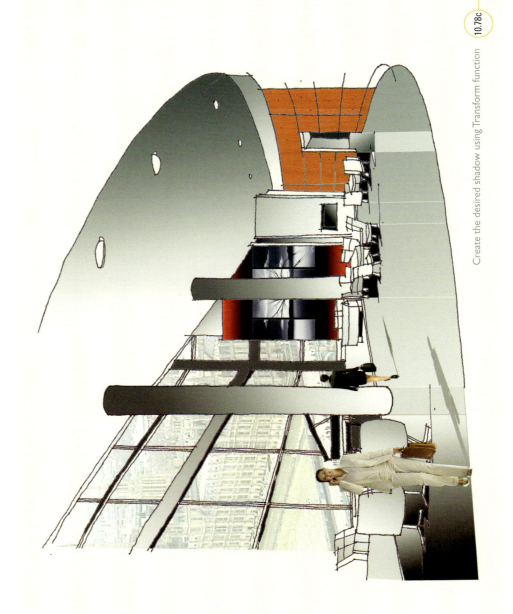

10.78c   Create the desired shadow using Transform function

ADDING SHADOWS ON MATERIALS AND SURFACES

If you have applied materials on a surface of the object, such as a wall, you still can apply gradient fill on top of it in order to create a shadow or change the value on that surface. The key point is to make that layer Step

Backward so you can apply gradient fill. Step Backward can be found on the History palette (see Figure 10.78e). To apply the gradient you use the same process as you did in the previous exercise. Figure 10.78e shows an example of applying gradient fill on top of the wood material on the wall.

In general, editing a PDF file of a line drawing in Photoshop is not hard. The transformed digital drawing presents the characteristics of both freehand sketching and digital drawing.

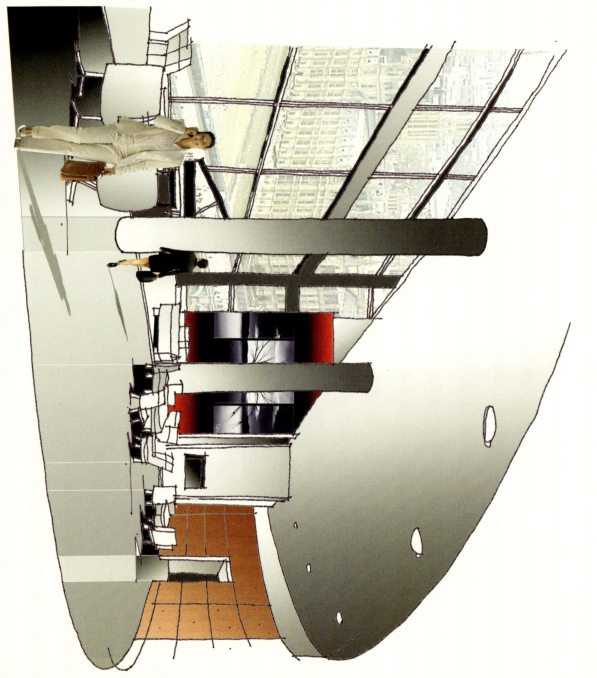

10.78d   Apply gradient fill to the wood material on the wall

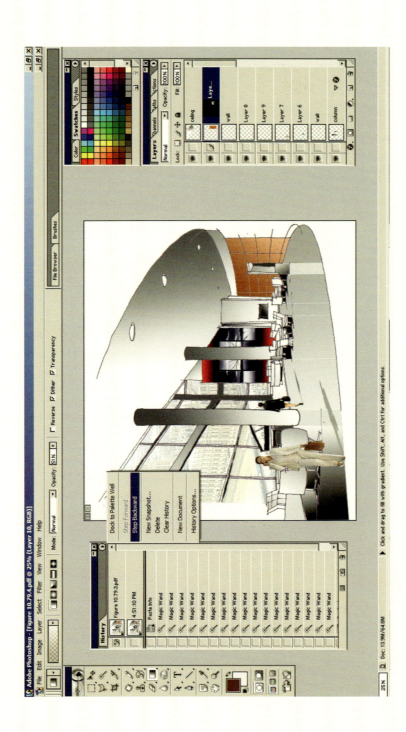

Location of Step Backward in History palette

10.78e

A COMPARISON OF THE CHARACTERISTICS OF FREEHAND DRAWING AND A TRANSFORMED DIGITAL DRAWING

In order to compare the two styles of drawing, let us first examine the basic characteristics of each.

Characteristics of Freehand Drawing

1. *Presents the sense of "human" touch with "imperfection" marks and uneven lines.* The freehand sketching process is an eye-mind-hand coordination process. Lines made in this way are not "perfect." They naturally embody tendencies and aberrations. It is this imperfection that reveals a sense of style and the human factor.

2. *Presents the process of creative thinking.* The ideas come directly from the designer through pencil or marker strokes. As the mind behind these strokes becomes more confident and engaged, the lines and marks tend to progress from tentative, aimless lines towards determined and firm graphic design solutions. Such lines and drawings record the designer's instant mindset at the moment when the ideas are generated.

3. *Presents unique individual manner and sketching style.* Experts can identify a writer's handwriting by different characteristics and style. Since the eye-mind-hand coordination and different personalities set the drawings apart, freehand drawings can be identified in individual sketching styles from the way lines, marks, and strokes were made.

Characteristics of Transformed Digital Drawing

1. *Maintains the sense of human touch by keeping freehand-drawn lines and marks.* Since the original sketch was scanned, the characteristics of freehand sketching are kept. All the "imperfections" are shown in the digital drawings. In addition to scanning line drawings, marker strokes, or colored pencil strokes can be scanned into a PDF file as well, in order to represent a more human touch.

2. *Presents the sense of realism by using the real materials and landscaping.* Real materials and landscaping from images retrieved from the Internet are used in this format. These JPEG files can be modified in Photoshop. Attaching these materials to a drawing makes the drawing more realistic.

3. *Presents the sense of sophistication by using the functions of computer software.* Many functions of Photoshop, such as the Paint Bucket tool, Gradient tool, Dodge tool, and Burn tool can fill in different colors and adjust darkness and brightness in the drawing. The changes made by these functions in Photoshop make the drawing look more sophisticated.

In summary, a transformed digital drawing is a hybrid of a freehand sketch and a digital drawing. It not only maintains the characteristics of freehand sketching, but also presents all the characteristics of digital drawing.

The following two exercises focus on creating digital drawings in both interior and exterior perspective. One special feature in the following exercises is to bring real trees, signage, and sky into the perspectives.

CREATING DIGITAL DRAWINGS FOR INTERIOR PERSPECTIVES—BRING IN SIGNAGE AND LANDSCAPING

10.5

Figures10.81 and 10.82 show two interior perspectives that were created with Photoshop from the drawings in Figures 10.79 and 10.80, respectively. The process is as same as previously described. The special feature of these digital drawings is that trees and signage were brought into them.

The following is the procedure to add trees or signage into your perspective:

1. Open up a tree image (Figure 10.83) or signage image (Figure 10.84) in either PDF or JPEG format in Photoshop.

2. Use the Rectangular Marquee tool to select the image, for example, a tree (Figure 10.85).

3. Copy the tree image. You can access the Copy command from the Edit pull-down menu. Then adjust the size of the tree or signage by using Transform as described earlier.

4. Open up your perspective drawing in Photoshop, such as in Figure 10.82. Paste the tree image or signage into your perspective.

5. Use the Move tool to put the tree or signage at the location you want.

6. When you paste multiple trees into your drawing, the size of the trees should be different due to the perspective effect. Therefore, you need to use the Transform command to reduce the tree size. Transform can be found in the Edit pull-down menu.

7. After you bring in trees, you can create shadows as described in this chapter.

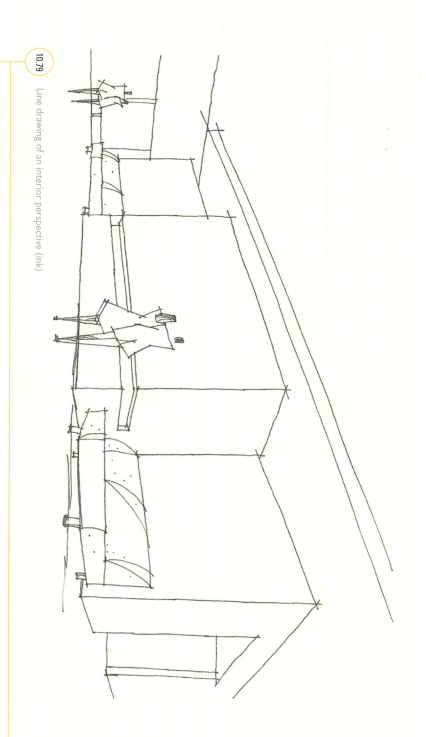

10.80

Line drawing of an interior perspective (Photoshop, ink)

10.79

Line drawing of an interior perspective (ink)

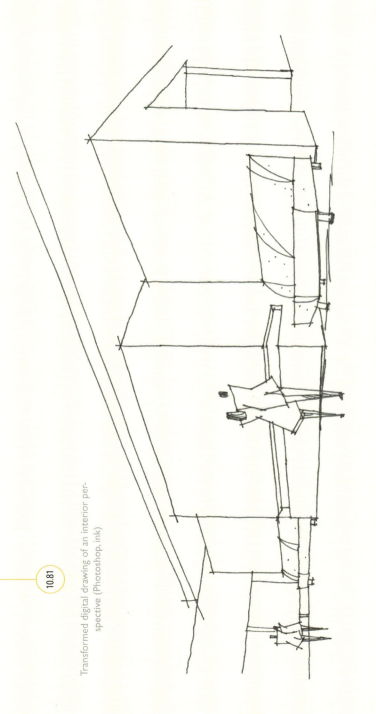

10.81

Transformed digital drawing of an interior perspective (Photoshop, ink)

10.82 Transformed digital drawing of an interior perspective

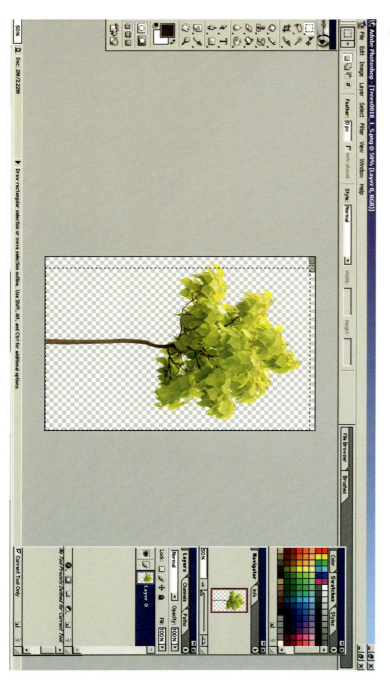

Use Rectangular Marquee tool to bring an image into a drawing

10.83

Tree image

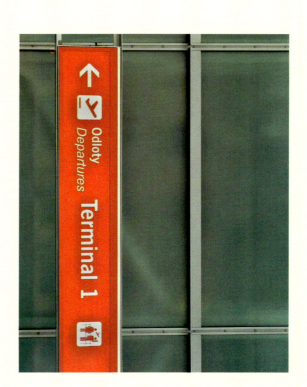

10.84

Signage (Photo © Shutterstock)

The following two examples show a line drawing edited in Photoshop (Figures 10.86 and 10.89). The blue sky image was downloaded from the Internet (Figure 10.88). You can simply use Copy and Paste to add the blue sky to your perspective drawing. The procedure is as same as described in Exercise 10.5. Figures 10.87 and 10.90 show another freehand exterior perspective sketch enlivened by its transformation into a digital drawing.

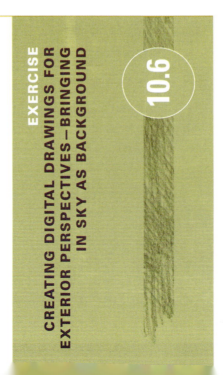

EXERCISE

CREATING DIGITAL DRAWINGS FOR EXTERIOR PERSPECTIVES – BRINGING IN SKY AS BACKGROUND

10.6

10.86   Line drawing of an office building (ink)

10.87   Transformed digital drawing of an office building (Photoshop, ink)

Sky image (Photo © iStockphoto) 10.88

● In order to keep as many freehand drawing characteristics as possible, you can add some ink strokes or marker strokes, such as freehand-drawn trees or plants before you scan your drawing to a PDF file.

● In that way, the transformed digital drawing will have freehand marks as well as simulate real materials.

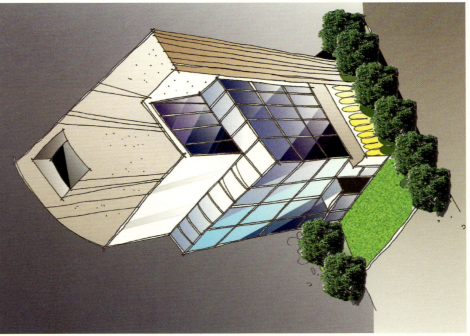

Transformed digital drawing of an office building (Photoshop, ink) 10.90

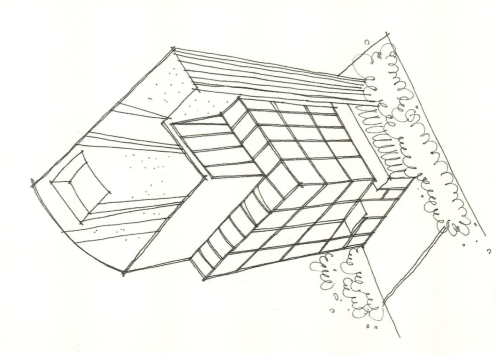

Line drawing of an office building (ink) 10.89

SUMMARY

In this chapter, you:

● Were introduced to the characteristics of freehand sketching.

● Learned to make the transition from freehand drawing to digital drawing.

● Were introduced to how to transform freehand drawing to digital format.

● Learned the procedure of editing digital images with Photoshop.

● Learned different characteristics of freehand drawing and digital drawing.

● Were introduced to how to bring in entourage and sky photos as backgrounds to drawings.

The very first step of transforming a sketch from freehand to digital is to scan a freehand drawing into a PDF file with a scanner. Keeping the characteristics of freehand sketching is the beauty of a perfectly executed digital drawing transformation. In order to keep the "imperfections" of a freehand drawing, you need to be loose and confident with your lines, marks, and strokes. In general, the digital image editing process is not very hard. You need to scan line drawings to prepare them for Photoshop. Use Google search to find JPEG files in order to incorporate simulations of real materials into the final digital drawing.

KEY TERMS

Burn Tool	Floor Plan	Marquee Tool
Copy	Gradient Tool	Paint Bucket Tool	Perspectives
Dodge Tool	Isometric view	Paste	Polygonal Lasso Tool
Entourage	Layer	Paste Into	Scanner
EPS File	Magic Wand	PDF File	Transform

1. The purpose of this exercise is to help you to practice the techniques described in this chapter and improve your skills of transforming a floor plan created by hand to a more professional-looking presentation floor plan. You will need to download images of materials and trees from the Internet for this exercise.

- Use your Sharpie to trace the floor plan as shown in Figure 10.91 on marker paper. Keep the characteristics of freehand sketching, which means free and loose strokes.
- Scan the drawing to a PDF or EPS file.
- You can decide what materials you are going to use on the floor plan; for example, carpet could be used in an office work area and terrazzo could be used in the reception area.
- Use Photoshop to edit the drawing by using gradient or solid fills, as well as bringing some trees or other foliage into your drawing.
- Add shadows on the floor plan in order to create contrast.
- Add background to the drawing as well.

2. This exercise is intended to help you practice the techniques described in this chapter and improve your skills when transforming freehand interior elevation drawings to digital ones, incorporating some real materials and background. Download images of materials and background from the Internet before you start the process.

- Use your Sharpie to trace the interior elevation as shown in Figure 10.92 on marker paper. Keep the characteristics of freehand sketching, which means free and loose lines and strokes.
- Scan the drawing to a PDF or EPS file.

continued from previous page

- Decide what materials you are going to use in the interior elevation, as well as what image you want to use as a background. For example, you may use wood for the receptionist's desk, and you may use brick on the bulkhead. You also can bring in an image for an exterior view visible through a window.

- Use Photoshop to edit the drawing by using gradient or solid fills, in addition to adding materials and background images.

- Add shadows on the interior perspective in order to create the contrast.

3. The purpose of this exercise is to help you practice the techniques described in this chapter and improve your skills of transforming freehand-drawn interior perspectives to digital drawings. You will need to download images of materials and background from the Internet before you start the process.

- Use your Sharpie to trace the floor plan as shown in Figure 10.93 on marker paper. Keep the characteristics of freehand sketching, which means free and loose lines and strokes.

- Scan the drawing to a PDF or EPS file.

- Decide what materials you are going to use for this interior perspective, as well as what image you want to use as a background showing through a big glass window.

- Use Photoshop to edit the drawing by using gradient or solid fills, as well as adding materials and background images to your drawing. Bringing in an image as an exterior view behind the curtain wall is important for this exercise.

- Add shadows on the interior elevation in order to create contrast.

4. This exercise is intended to help you to practice the techniques described in this chapter and improve your skills when transforming freehand-drawn interior isometric drawing to digital with the inclusion of some materials and trees. First download the images you want to incorporate into this drawing from the Internet.

- Use your Sharpie to trace the isometric drawing as shown in Figure 10.94 on marker paper. Keep the characteristics of freehand sketching, which means free and loose lines and strokes.

- Scan the drawing to a PDF or EPS file.

- Decide on what materials you are going to use in this interior isometric drawing.

- Use Photoshop to edit the drawing by using gradient or solid fills, as well as adding materials and trees into your drawing.

- Add shadows on the isometric drawing in order to create contrast.

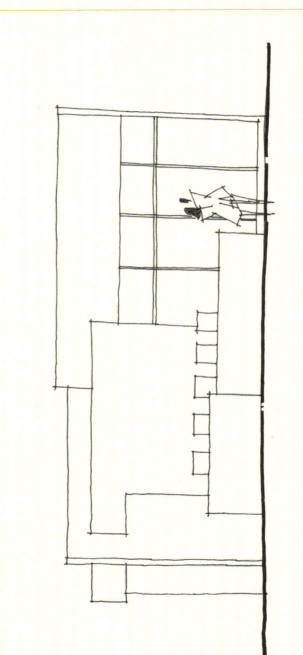

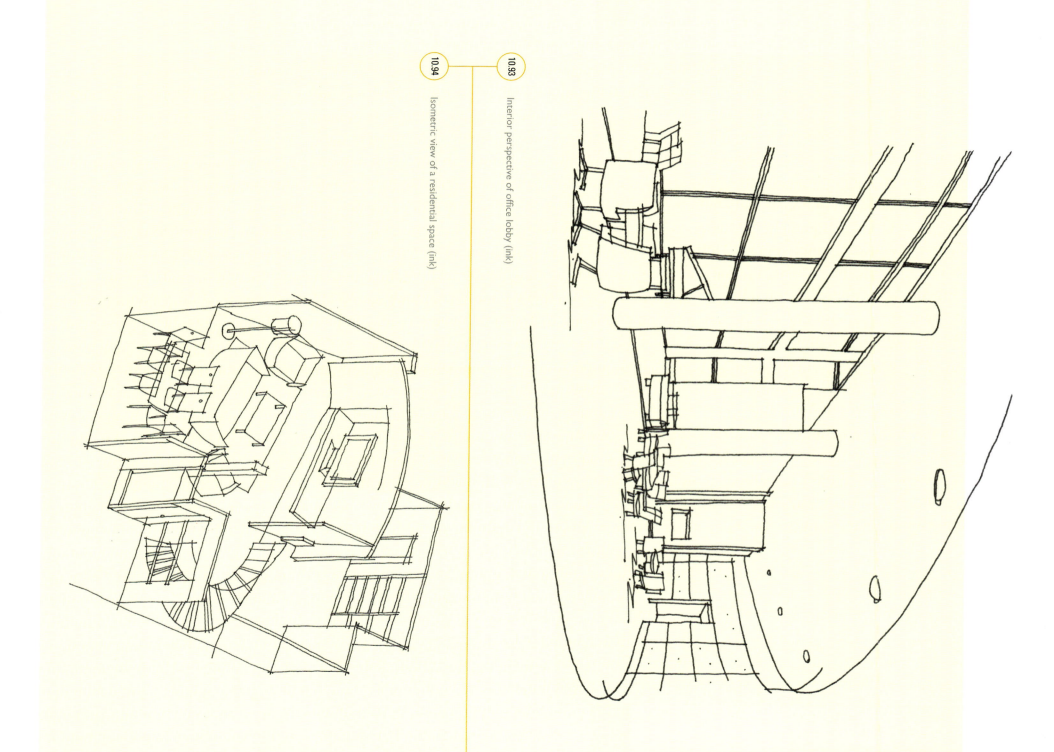

Isometric view of a residential space (ink)

Interior perspective of office lobby (ink)